DISABILITY RIGHTS GUIDE

WITHDRAWN

DISABILITY RIGHTS GUIDE

Practical Solutions To Problems Affecting People With Disabilities

by
Charles D. Goldman, Esq.

Media Publishing
Lincoln, Nebraska

Library of Congress #90-63203
ISBN 0-939644-77-0

Printed in the United States of America

MEDIA PUBLISHING
2440 'O' Street, Suite 202
Lincoln, Nebraska 68510-1125

Daniel, Lisa, Jennifer, and Michael
Here's to you my loves!

May you too grow more involved.
May you grow beyond your dreams.

As always, love, Dad

TABLE OF CONTENTS

Author's Note xi

Preface xiii

Acknowledgments xv

Introduction . . . .

CHAPTER 1: Attitudinal Barriers
Introduction 5
Misconceptions: Demystifying the Problems 7
   1. Disability Is Inability
   2. Persons With Disabilities Cannot Speak For Themselves
   3. Persons Without Disabilities Have A Duty To Take Care Of
      Persons With Disabilities
   4. All Persons With Disabilities Are Hearing Impaired
   5. All Persons With Hearing Impairments Can Read Lips Perfectly
      And That Corrects Everything
   6. All Persons With Visual Impairments Read Braille
   7. No One Really Uses The Parking Spaces Designated For Persons
      With Disabilities
   8. It Is Rude To Ask Persons With Disabilities If They Need
      Help (The Hesitation Or Big City Syndrome)
   9. All Persons With Learning Disabilities Have The Same Problem
  10. Mental Retardation Is Catching And Dangerous To The
      Neighborhood
  11. All Persons In Wheelchairs Have The Same Problems
      And Must Stay In Their Chairs
  12. Persons With Disabilities Are Sick And Unhappy
  13. A Ramp—Even One At The Back Door Means A Building
      Is "Accessible"
  14. Aids Is Transmitted By Casual Contact
  15. All Disabled Individuals Are Alike (The Monolithic Model)
Language: Observations, "Do's and Don'ts" 13
Doing It Right: Pointers for Positive Interactions . . 16
A Final Note 19

CHAPTER 2: Employment

Introduction 21
Federal Law 22
State and Local Laws 39
Incentives 44
Reasonable Accommodations: A Sample Policy . . . 45
Recruiting Techniques 48
Questions That Can Be Asked 50
A Few No-Nos 51
A Final Note 52

CHAPTER 3: Accessibility: Public Accommodations and Architectural Barriers

Introduction 53
Federal Mandates for Accessibility 55
A Few Final Notes In Passing From The Rehab Act . . 66
State Laws 67
Compliance Incentives 69
Coping: Points to Remember 70
Applicability of Access Code Form 72
Approaching Access Standards:
Technical Considerations Form 74
A Final Note 78

CHAPTER 4: Housing

Introduction 79
Federal Law 80
State Laws 89
Adaptable/Accessible Housing 92
Adaptability/Accessibility Functionality Checklist . . 93
More Practical Points 94
A Final Note 96

CHAPTER 5: Education

Introduction 97
Application of the Rehabilitation Act 99
Individuals with Disabilities Education Act 104

Americans with Disabilities Act 110
A Final Note 111
Sample Special Education Policy Statement 112
Sample Continuum of Education Placements Chart . .118
Sample Policy Statement on Procedural Rights . . .119

CHAPTER 6: Transportation
Introduction 123
Driving 125
Federal Law and Regulatory Efforts: Rehabilitation Act
and Mass Transit; Americans with Disabilities Act . 127
Subways 130
Commuter Rail 131
Rail 132
Americans with Disabilies Act 133
Air Travel 137
Highways 139
Transportation Planning:
A Tool for a Defined Community 140
Sample Needs Form 141
A Final Note 143
"Driving & Epilepsy" Chart 143

Summing Up 151

Glossary 153
Words, And Parts Thereof, For The Wise 153
By The Numbers 164

APPENDIX I: State by State Guide: Laws and Contacts . 165

APPENDIX II: Federal Contacts 203

APPENDIX III: AIDS. 213

APPENDIX IV: Technology Related Assistance 245

About the Author 254

Author's Note

This book is intended for all people, non-disabled or disabled, who address problems of persons with physical or mental limitations, what are popularly referred to as handicaps or disabilities. In fact, throughout this book the point is made to emphasize that we are interacting with persons, persons who may have physical or mental disabilities. However, the statutes and regulations are commonly written in terms of "handicapped persons," "handicapped individuals," or "handicapped children." Accordingly, those terms are used in this text as linkages to the official materials.

More recently Congress has framed laws using terms such as "individual with disability." This is recognition of the primacy of the person, not the disability. The terms "person" or "individual" with disability, interchangeable terms here, are coming into most widespread usage in the laws and in everyday life. The conceptual framework and complementary practical solutions are provided to address issues of attitudinal barriers, employment, accessibility, housing, education, and transportation. The appendices are keys into the state and federal systems. There is also information on AIDS and technology related assistance centers.

Preface

The telephone rang Saturday morning. "Goldman," intoned the caller, "It's going to pass. Start writing."

Disabled sociologist and guru, Mary Jane Owen, had spent the past week lobbying for the Americans with Disabilities Act. Now victory seemed at hand. Persons with physical and mental disabilities were being afforded full responsibilities and protections under federal civil rights laws. It was time to write an update.

Easing back in my chair, after rechecking my children's soccer schedule and realizing there was that rarest of all commodities, time to contemplate, I picked up a legal pad, and began making notes:

— ADA (Americans with Disabilities Act)
— Civil Rights Restoration Act
— Fair Housing Amendments
— Air Carrier Access Act
— AIDS
— State Updates
— Regs-504, Fair Housing
— Cases

A few minutes work confirmed the thesis: ADA was the crowning jewel in a list of substantive changes since publication of my first guide on disability rights in late 1987. The practical materials previously presented were now even more valuable since the laws had been broadened to embrace more employers, places, and services. The nondiscrimination mandates in federal laws had been made more inclusive. More people had to cope with the mandates.

Conceptualization of this next edition had begun.

On the "if it ain't broken, don't fix it" theory much of what was presented in the first edition has been retained. There has been editing with the major additions and revisions to make the updated text reflect the changes in the laws. State laws and contacts

and federal contacts in the first two appendices have been updated. More information on AIDS is added, especially in Appendix III. Appendix IV has been added to identify assistive technology centers. New terms from the new laws enhance the Glossary.

As I pondered my notes, I doodled an arrow, pointing upward.
My meditation of a few minutes was punctuated by the urgings of
my youngest child. "C'mon, dad. We have to go to my game," he
pleaded. (Lawyer's children learn early on the value of pleading
their causes.) "Besides," he said looking at my papers, "now that
it is so important, people'll want to do it right."

This new edition is to continue to help people who want to "do
it right," as we in society keep evolving our pluralistic culture to
include full participation by persons with disabilities.

In Washington, D.C., there is a maxim that "Where you stand
on an issue depends on where you sit." When I first became
involved on the disability issues, I was a federal government
attorney ensuring that buildings were accessible. Now, as a
private practitioner, I grapple with real, live people on a daily
basis — their employment, education, housing, independent living
problems. The people I have encountered have helped me grow
and have molded my perspective.

My experiences in disability issues have not shaken and, if
anything, have reinforced my fundamental belief that the law is
for the people. Despite the mystique about the "law," we are, in
reality, a society of people. We people solve our problems, we in
turn shape and help the "law" evolve.

May this book help us, as a society, continue to grow past our
problems.

Acknowledgments

The author wishes to express deep thanks to the many persons who have been of assistance. Darla Fera and Kathy Dunten, my editors from the *Handicapped Requirements Handbook*, who got me started writing, and Robert Silverstein, my former colleague, gave me trusted technical aid. My law clerk, Lisa Lieber, spent hours researching state codes. Linda Messman at Media Publishing kept me on task. My clients gave me the experiences about which to write and the sense to write. My children helped with their experiences, moral support, my grammar and the cover design. They were especially helpful in making sure this book was in English, not legalese. Thanks.

Introduction

Several years ago when I first went into private practice of law, a good friend, who happens to be my dentist, Dr. Frank Maglio, asked me if I would be specializing in disability rights. Seeing my quizzical expression he continued on, as all good dentists do when they are standing over you and your mouth is full of their instruments, observing very astutely, "What's happened? We don't hear that much about the issues any more? Where have all the people gone?"

The observation rang true and made me pause (not that I had too much of an opportunity to be very articulate, given the circumstances).

Until recently we have not had many dramatic confrontations. The Rehabilitation Act and its civil rights mandates not to discriminate against qualified handicapped persons has been adopted and is being implemented gradually. Buildings are being made more accessible under federal, state and local accessibility laws. The Education for All Handicapped Children Act has spurred state laws which have brought children into the public school systems. There are state and local civil rights laws that protect the rights of persons with disabilities to enjoy public places and obtain housing. These laws were enacted as part of the national thrust for civil rights for persons with disabilities, which reached a new peak in 1990 with the enactment of the Americans with Disabilities Act.

It is far more common to see a person in a wheelchair on the subway in Washington, D.C., than to see a person picketing the subway authority. It is increasingly more common to see persons who are hearing impaired in an office or to have persons who are visually impaired engaged in meaningful jobs.

In a nutshell, the past two decades have witnessed an evolution to an era where the aura is one of implementation. We have gone from "Burn, Baby, Burn" to "Learn, Baby, Learn" to "Earn, Baby, Earn."

As a whole, in part because of the laws discussed in this book as well as for generic evolutionary reasons, American society has become far more accepting of the 43 million persons with disabilities.

The Vietnam War created a new generation of veterans, persons who came home to rebuild the American dream they had left behind. Because of advanced medical technology, many came home who would not have come home from previous wars. Disabled veterans have been at the forefront of the movements for laws guaranteeing civil rights — protections for which they had fought for overseas and which they thought they had when they left.

Persons with disabilities were able to have laws enacted because others had struggled before them. In the 1960s the civil rights movement shocked our country into adopting protections for minorities. Women's rights entered the legal arena in the very early 1970s. These developments facilitated the adoption of the protections for persons with disabilities.

In 1963, the March on Washington led by Reverend Dr. Martin Luther King, Jr. was critical in leading to the Civil Rights Act of 1964. The 20th Anniversary March in 1983 showed how things had changed for persons with disabilities. In 1963, the disability community had no presence at the March. In 1983, the persons with disabilities were there as full participants.

Years ago, persons with disabilities would be hidden away, sheltered by parents or institutionalized. I recall touring a home in the Maryland suburbs of Washington when my realtor called for me to come to the top level. There, on the fourth floor of this charming old home, was a completely accessible bathroom — guard rails and grab bars around the toilet, the sink, and in the shower. The only problem was that it was impossible for a person with a mobility impairment — classically, a person in a wheelchair — to reach that upper level. It was only accessible by several flights of steps. While we never found out why the house was so designed, the incident struck me as a sad reminder of how persons with disabilities were kept out of the mainstream, hidden away on fourth floors or other equally less visible domains. I cannot fathom such a situation recurring. A slew of social welfare programs have been established over the past several years. While there were special schools for blind and deaf students at least as far back as the 1860s and President Lincoln, "modern" protections and rehabilitation programs for persons with disabilities really got going after World War I. The last 20 years have been a period of exponential growth in terms of the proliferation of programs, disability advocacy, rights, and organizations, as well as societal recognition of persons with disabilities as persons. In 1988 both political parties, Republican and Democrat, courted the votes of persons with disabilities.

In 1988, after extensive demonstrations by deaf students, Gallaudet University installed the first hearing impaired President in the 120 year history of the leading school in the Nation for educating deaf and hearing impaired persons. In 1990 disabled persons and their allies lobbied and demonstrated in vintage 1960s/1970s form to help achieve enactment of the Americans with Disabilities Act.

The critical starting premise is that persons with disabilities — physical or mental — are just that — persons. A second key precept is that we must remember that, lamentably, it could be any of us at any time. Disability asks no questions before it strikes. No one checks politics before the car crashes or the baby is born with congenital defects. The natural loss of hearing or vision is part of life.

As a society we are living and working longer and seeking to keep on participating. We ascribe a positive value to such active participation. Retirement laws have changed and older persons increasingly have stayed in the mainstream. As they do, unfortunately their limitations stay with them and we make accommodations with amplified telephone systems or big print reading materials. As people grow older they grow less physically able, but most retain mental acuity.

In brief, persons with disabilities are off the fourth floor and here to stay, not only as persons with disabilities, but as active members of society. As such, they seek, as did others before them, to be integral active participants.

In this book I discuss the key parameters of the legal-social fabric of participants. I discuss the issues — accessibility, housing, employment, education, and transportation — from the practical perspective of techniques to address and solve problems. These are the real bricks and mortar barriers that people with disabilities encounter as they weave the fabric of their daily lives.

However, I begin with what is said to be the biggest barrier of them all. While it persistently manifests itself, it is usually invisible and permeates our language and culture. It is the root base of all of the other problems. It is the attitudinal barrier which tells us how to feel about persons with disabilities and frequently governs our interactions with them. Telling a Black person to "sit in the back of the bus," is akin to saying to a person with disabilities, "keep off the bus because it has no lift for your wheelchair or crutches."

In this first chapter we establish the personal mind set for recognizing and remembering that persons with disabilities are persons.

Chapter 1

ATTITUDINAL BARRIERS

Introduction

It is the biggest barrier of them all. While it is never written into the laws or regulations, it permeates our daily living. It affects all of our daily lives. It affects how we feel about ourselves and how we feel about others. It comes out in the design of buildings as well as job interviews.

It is the attitudes we have towards persons with disabilities. It is what we think and what we feel about ourselves and towards the person who has a vision or hearing impairment or walks with a cane or is in a wheelchair. While there may be physical barriers in a building which can be restructured or a job questionnaire that can be redone, by far the largest task is to ascertain and weed out the hidden biases, both the innate and the developed, which impact on how we feel and how we act when addressing issues of persons with disabilities or interacting with them.

Laws and regulations can tell people what they must do and the consequences, both positive and negative, of adherence to such laws. But there are no laws which can dictate how a person feels when carrying out those responsibilities. And very commonly, it is truly a matter of perspective.

Several years ago I had spent the day in Baltimore, Maryland, at one of the annual summer festivals hosted by city leaders. These are highly ethnic events, featuring diverse cultures, such as Polish, German, Italian, or Jewish, to which the crowds throng to soak up the atmosphere, taste the food and enjoy. While I am a little fuzzy as to whether it was the Jewish or Italian festival, I recall the vehement gestures and total body language with which the participants communicated with one another. Many of the spectators, including me, pointed that out to their children. Part of the attraction was seeing people talk with their hands.

Later that day I had to go to a shopping mall. Inevitably, one of my children wanted a drink, and we got in line. The vendor was in a state of shock as the person in front of us was attempting to order food using sign language! Where earlier in the day at the ethnic festival, using your hands to communicate was part of the attraction, a veritable cultural badge of honor, the same method was now a business horror for the vendor.

For ethnic persons to use their hands was fine. People came from miles around to see that. But for deaf persons ordering food, using their hands was unsportsmanlike conduct and a terrifying penalty.

The day has remained with me over the years because it brought home to me dramatically how we as a society approach problems and the values we attach to certain conduct.

Not all food stories are bad. I recall attending a meeting in a Chinese restaurant in downtown Washington shortly after the election of Jimmy Carter. We were there that cold November evening at the behest of our hostess, a charming southern lady, Peggy Smith, who had been quite active in the election campaign. She was now devoting her efforts to maximizing people's participation in the Inaugural events and hoopla. She had never worked with persons with disabilities. Now she sat in the middle of several persons with different disabilities and their advocates. The preliminary chitchat was proceeding when Peggy raised her voice, and with the aplomb of a veteran politician, drawled, "Hey, you all, what do we do to do the Inauguration right for you? How do we make the Inauguration good for handicapped people? What do we say? How do we do it right?"

For too long it was done wrong and misconceptions about persons with disabilities abounded and were fostered. Now that things are changing, the interactions are more positive, and there are new buzz words, indigenous to disability rights issues. This chapter focuses on saying and doing it right. Positive dialogue and positive interactions will be major thrusts in avoiding problems. For too long much wrong was done, and stereotypical misconceptions persisted about a host of things. In this chapter, several of these errors are highlighted and put to rest. The focus then shifts to the language of disability and to behavioral techniques to apply the language correctly.

Misconceptions: Demystifying The Problems

The historic pattern of excluding persons with disabilities from the mainstream of society served to create and perpetuate certain myths or misconceptions about people with disabilities. The residue of such misperceptions remains with us today. Yet in the later stages of the twentieth century these notions really have no place.

1. Disability Is Inability

The ill-fostered illusion is that because of a physical or mental impairment the person cannot do particular things like work, cook, or enjoy a social activity. Persons with disabilities do not sit around bemoaning their fates. They are in society as participants. Many persons with disabilities view their limitations as an inconvenience. This is indicative of their self images as goers and doers who carry on regular lives. Merely being in a wheelchair or having hearing or vision problems does not and should not be viewed as preclusion from working, enjoying life, or being full-fledged persons in society. Installation of a hearing impaired President of Gallaudet University in 1988 was a classic refutation of this myth. Dr. I. King Jordan is an accomplished educator and administrator, who happens to be hearing-impaired.

2. Persons With Disabilities Cannot Speak For Themselves

If a person with disabilities and a person without disabilities go into a restaurant, there is a real possibility that the server will ask the person without disabilities what the person with disabilities wants. This once happened to a blind colleague and his wife. When the waiter asked his wife, "What does he want?" the rejoinder came from my blind colleague: "And he wants a steak, too!" This was shown dramatically in the popular movie "Children of a Lesser God" when the hearing character, portrayed by William Hurt, was asked what the deaf person, Marlee Matlin, wanted for dinner. This perception is an offshoot of the old myth that it was up to society (sic. the able-bodied) to take care of the poor, downtrodden disabled.

3. Persons Without Disabilities Have A Duty To Take Care Of Persons With Disabilities

Some persons with disabilities may require attendant care and additional services. However, overwhelmingly, and increasingly, persons with disabilities can and do take care of themselves and seek to do just that. This third myth reflects the paternalism which was fostered when all persons with disabilities were viewed as "cripples" and predates modern technology and the evolution of modern communication devices as well as community independent living centers and group homes.

4. All Persons With Disabilities Are Hearing Impaired

Have you ever noticed the voice level of persons who are not disabled when they talk to persons with disabilities, even those without a hearing impairment? Invariably, it is several decibels louder than when speaking with a person who is not disabled. It is as if being visually impaired or being in a wheelchair also automatically has caused the loss of hearing or lack of understanding. A variation on this theme is seen at political gatherings where all the persons with disabilities are herded to a special section—adjacent to the band. Those persons in the group who weren't hearing impaired before the action are so impaired afterward. In truth, the reasons for disabilities are disparate and there is usually no interrelationship or multiple disability.

5. All Persons With Hearing Impairments Can Read Lips Perfectly And That Corrects Everything

All of us to some extent rely on lip reading to understand what people are saying. But too often the assumption is made that all persons with hearing impairments can understand everything being said by reading lips. Experts believe that, at the very best, a person who reads lips can understand 60 to 70 percent (and often less than 50%) of the words spoken. Think about how important body language and facial expressions are as part of the total communications we experience. Try turning off the sound on your television and see how much of the dialogue and meaning you understand.

Little words can mean everything. Consider this example: "The prisoner is in the charge of the guard."

Now, as revised: "The prisoner is in the charge of the guard."

Hearing aids and lip reading do not restore perfect hearing. They only serve to lessen the severity of the loss.

6. All Persons With Visual Impairments Read Braille

Braille is a communication system for persons with visual impairments. It is based on raised dots on paper which are aligned to make letters and numbers. Conceptually, it is analogous to sign language for persons with hearing impairments. Not all persons with low vision or visual impairments know Braille. At the most, 15 percent of persons with vision impairments read Braille. Many persons with vision impairments use tapes and other mechanical devices, including reading machines and computers that talk.

7. No One Really Uses The Parking Spaces Designated For Persons With Disabilities

This is sometimes known as the "I'll only be a minute" syndrome. Parking is especially critical to persons who are mobility impaired. Too often people who are not disabled will park in the spaces designated for persons with disabilities which is properly located near the accessible entrance. Believing they will be brief and that no one will mind, these people dash in and out. Local police departments are increasingly active in enforcing the local ordinances prohibiting parking in the spaces designated except by properly identified vehicles, thereby shattering the myth with a basic negative incentive. A cousin of mine saw a car parked in a designated space and doing his citizen's duty, though not a member of the constabulary, dashed off this note: "It's for PHYSI-CALLY handicapped."

8. It Is Rude To Ask Persons With Disabilities If They Need Help (The Hesitation or Big City Syndrome)

The person who is not disabled sees a person with a disability who needs help, for example someone lost on a street corner, and hesitates "getting involved" for fear of being offensive. In truth, a person who looks like he needs help, either at a social gathering or on the street, may need help. If you ask politely, you will not be wrong. It should not matter whether or not the person in apparent need is disabled. Too often people are afraid to inquire for fear of upsetting the other person. It is not impertinent to inquire with dignity.

9. All Persons With Learning Disabilities Have The Same Problem

Learning disabilities manifest themselves in various ways. Some persons transpose digits when they write because they read them differently. This is a symptom of dyslexia. Other persons have difficulty distinguishing left from right. Some persons have reading comprehension difficulties or attention span deficits.

Some persons may have multiple learning disabilities. Each individual with a learning disability and each learning disability must be addressed individually. They are not all alike.

10. Mental Retardation Is Catching And Dangerous To The Neighborhood

This is known as the "contagious syndrome." Mental retardation is a condition of delayed, limited development in learning. It is a permanent, organic condition limited to the individual. There is no evidence that it is contagious. In these respects mental retardtion is similar to other physical disabilities such as epilepsy, emphysema, and muscular dystrophy. Nevertheless, inevitably, there is a hue and cry when a group home for persons who are mentally retarded is proposed. In fact, the residents of the home often function quite well as members of the community, their limitations notwithstanding. There is no evidence that persons who are mentally retarded are "bad" neighbors. The United States Supreme Court has ruled that irrational, medically unfounded fears of contagiousness are intolerable.

11. All Persons In Wheelchairs Must Stay In Their Chairs And Have The Same Problems

The need to use wheelchairs, crutches, or other prostheses is individualized. Not all users of wheelchairs are paraplegics or quadriplegics. Not all are paralyzed. Depending upon such factors as a person's health, muscle strength, coordination, and the disabling condition, a person may have the strength and dexterity to transfer to chairs or seats in the home, at the job, or in automobiles. The individual may use a wheelchair but is not necessarily limited or "confined" to it.

12. Persons With Disabilities Are Sick And Unhappy

This may seem ridiculously obvious but, unfortunately, this myth persists. Stereotypical images linger and this is part of the residue from the times persons with disabilities were hidden away, the fourth floor type in the house I mentioned at the outset. In truth, persons with disabilities have all the emotions and feelings of their able-bodied cohorts in society. A cane, hearing aid, or prosthesis does not detract from the range and contents of a person's emotions. Many persons with physical limitations attributable to a particular condition have no additional health problems.

13. A Ramp—Even One At The Back Door—Means A Building Is "Accessible"

A structure is "accessible" if a person with a disability not only can approach and enter but can use the building as well, with dignity, independence, safely, and conveniently. Access, especially in new or renovated buildings, means going through the primary (main) entrance. Back door entrances for minorities were rejected decades ago as embodying stigmatizing, second class treatment. Back door entrances are likewise and equally unacceptable for persons with disabilities.

14. AIDS Is Transmitted By Casual Contact

The United States Surgeon General makes clear this is not the case. Intimate unsafe sexual contact or other bodily contact involving the passing of fluids or sharing of needles is how the AIDS virus is transmitted. Transmittal by casual contact is just a myth, not fact.

15. All Disabled Individuals Are Alike (The Monolithic Model)

This has been alluded to in Misconceptions 3, 4, 8, and 11. It is crucial to remember that the community of persons with disabilities is comprised of individuals with differing limitations — mobility, vision, hearing, mental, learning, communication, etc. There is no monolithic model or model disabled individual.

Language: Observations, "Do's And Don'ts"

The misconceptions we have about persons with disabilities come out in the ways we speak to and about such people. Over the past two decades, especially, there has been a growing awareness of the language of persons with disabilities.

In a nutshell, the language now in vogue reflects how increasingly positive persons with disabilities feel about themselves as participants in programs and society. Current language also demonstrates how persons with disabilities wish that society would view them as positive, contributing, independent persons.

The language of disability is evolving, much in the way language as a whole changes. In a totally different context things that were once "hip," "cool" or "sharp" are now "awesome." In a similar sense we recognize people as "Jewish," not "hymies." "Black" and "Afro-American" are acceptable whereas "Negro" has negative connotations. So, too, with the language of disability.

Persons with a physical or mental impairment or limitation are called persons with a disability, not handicapped. This underscores that the disabling condition may not be a limitation. The Americans with Disabilities Act was written in 1990 in terms of individuals with disabilities. When Congress extends the Rehabilitation Act in 1991 or 1992 it is expected that the terminology of that law will change from "handicapped individuals" to "individuals with disabilities."

If there are curb cuts or curb ramps, the person in a wheelchair can go from one street to the next, so mobility impairment is not a limitation. Harold Krents, a lawyer who was blind, encountered many difficult situations in which he was effectively excluded from his chosen profession. However, when he was a student during the 1965 blackout and the lights went out in his dormitory, his blindness became an advantage as he led his sighted, and newly limited, colleagues to safety. He knew the way in the dark. In the blackout, his "handicap" vanished and it was the "able-bodied" seeing students who were truly disabled for the first time.

The trend now is to focus our language and our interactions on the person, the individual. Recent laws and regulations do just that. So, too, must we in our interactions realize that the biggest "do" is to remember that the individual with a disability is first and foremost an individual, a person.

Do's And Don'ts

1. Always talk about people, not "the." Say "persons with disabilities." Do not say "the disabled."
2. Never use words like "cripple" ('crip'), "afflicted," "confined," "victim," "wheelchair-bound," "spastic," "invalid," "retard," or "gimp." These are all first class insults which may provoke an unwelcome response with a prosthesis.
3. The commonly preferred term to use to describe a person in a wheelchair or a person who uses crutches is "a person with a mobility impairment."
4. The term "person who is hearing impaired" is an acceptable way of describing a person with a hearing loss. If the person has no hearing, the person may be described as "profoundly hearing impaired" or "deaf." NEVER say "deaf and dumb." It is denigrating as well as not true.
5. "Person who is visually (or vision) impaired" is the commonly preferred term to describe a person with sight or vision problems and loss. A person who has no sight whatsoever may be described as "blind."
6. A person with two limbs paralyzed (usually the legs) is a person who is a paraplegic ("para"). A person whose four limbs are paralyzed is a quadraplegic ("quad").
7. "Seizure" is an acceptable term whereas "fit," "spells," or "spastic" should not be used.
8. A person with a muscular or neurological condition should be described as a person who has or who had the particular condition, e.g., a person who has muscular dystrophy or who had

a stroke. Do not describe the person as a "victim" or a "sufferer." That is a put down.

9. Persons who cannot speak or who cannot speak clearly should be described as "a person with a speech impairment" or as a person who cannot speak. Do not say "mute," "dumb," or "dummy."

10. The term "hidden disability" is used to refer to a disabling condition or an impairment which is not apparent from looking at a person. It is an acceptable way to describe a person who is hearing impaired, a person whose seizures are under control, or a person who has a prosthesis which is not visible.

11. The terms "idiot," "moron," "slow," "simple minded," "Mongoloid," or "deficient" should not be used. The correct term traditionally has been "mentally retarded," though now the term "mentally disabled" also is used.

12. "Emotionally disabled" is a new term coming into vogue to describe a person with mental illness or receiving psychological or psychiatric treatment. Do not use terms such as "psycho," "nut," or "former mental patient." "Physically challenged" is a new term being used for persons with physical disabilities.

13. The word "normal" is not viewed as a positive or even neutral word. The terms "able-bodied," "AB," or "TAB" are used to refer to able-bodied persons. The latter is not a reference to a soft drink but is an acronym for "temporarily able-bodied," designed to illustrate how fleetingly illusory health or an able body can be.

14. Don't say "handicapped toilet," "handicapped parking," or "disabled seating." The toilet, space, or seat are not limited. They are for use by persons with disabilities. The best way to refer to the item would be "accessible toilet," "parking for persons with disabilities," "accessible seating."

15. Avoid the cutesy adjectives when referring to a particular person with a disability. Words such as "brave," "courageous," or "inspirational" tend to foster the stereotypical myths (e.g., Misconception 12) that need to be dispelled.

16. Avoid phraseology like "AIDS victims" for the same reasons

noted under Dos and Don'ts No.8, above. It is lamentable that society has reverted to pitying and looking down on persons with AIDS.

17. "AIDS Carrier" is stigmatizing and reminiscent of the typhoid hysteria. The correct term, depending upon the person's condition is "person with AIDS" (noted as "PWA") or "HIV positive" (sometimes "HIV$^+$") person.

18. Remember you are interacting with individuals who may have a preference in how they are addressed. Remember to ask them. Remember it is the individual, the person, not their disability, with whom you are interacting.

Doing It Right: Pointers For Positive Interactions

As often as not, *how* we say things is just as important as *what* we say. Our body language and facial expressions are equally, if not more, important than the words used. In brief, the correct idea is to interact with the person with a disability in the same manner in which you interact with the person who does not have a disability. The following suggestions highlight common problems and human foibles.

1. Maintain eye contact, even if the person has no sight or a vision impairment. If you are engaged in a prolonged conversation with a person in a wheelchair, sit down to keep eye contact. Many people have difficulty making and maintaining eye contact. To prove it to yourself, walk down a crowded street and look the people in the eye. Notice how many look away.

2. The art of conversation works best when kept natural. Let the words flow along their routine course when talking with a person with a disability. If the correct terminology or usage is to say, "Did you see that?" or "Did you hear that?" then use those terms even if interacting with someone who may not have the particular sense to which your words refer. Don't hesitate or stumble around for words to compensate.

3. When talking with a person who is hearing impaired, talk to that person, not to any interpreter who may be present. If there is a need to reposition you or the interpreter, then the person with the hearing impairment will let it be known. This is also true when interacting with persons with other disabilities, such as a person who is blind or in a wheelchair. Talk to the person with whom you are interacting, not their prosthesis. Any physical limitation is no cause to change the pattern of interaction.

4. In a group discussion involving a person who is hearing impaired, remember the interpreter can only sign for one speaker at a time. Therfore, avoid interruptions and cross-conversations.

5. When talking with a person who is in a wheelchair or who has crutches, NEVER touch the crutches or the wheelchair unless you intend to touch the person. If you touch the crutches or wheelchair, you ARE touching the person. The person does not need your support. Crutches and wheelchairs are extensions of the persons using them.

6. As you get to know a particular person with disabilities, listen to how he describes himself. Ask the person what words or phrases you can or cannot use to describe him.

7. Be especially patient when talking with a person with a speech impairment. That person wants you to hear his words as badly as you want to hear them. There is nothing so frustrating as being unable to finish your sentences, whether you are speech impaired or not. It does take a bit of patience but when you let the person speak, you hear him out in the same manner you wish to be heard — completely.

8. Use a normal conversational tone as a general rule. There is no reason to shout when talking with a person who is visually or mobility impaired (Misconception 4, above). Ask a person who is hearing impaired how much you need to raise your voice. Also, remember to keep your hands away from your mouth.

9. Do not ask a person when or how they became disabled. You do not ask people of other minorities when they became

Jewish, Black, or Hispanic. When and how a person became disabled is irrelevant. If you have some reason to know about their condition, then ask the question in terms of their functioning. For example, if you are worried about a visitor who is mobility impaired and you do not have a grade level entrance but do have a small step, ask the person if they can manage that threshold or whether you need some form of portable ramp. If you inquire with polite dignity about the function, all should be fine.

10. Use conventional conversational words and phrases that are appropriate to your background as well as the subject. Persons with disabilities are just as intelligent/stupid as other persons. A person's blindness or use of a wheelchair should not occasion a return to "Run, Spot, Run," "Fun with Dick and Jane," language. A physical handicap is not cause for mental simplification.

11. If you do not understand what a person is saying, ask him to repeat it. This happens with deaf persons who have limited voice use as well as with other persons who have speech impairments, e.g., persons with cerebral palsy. It is perfectly acceptable to politely ask a person — whether or not they have a disability — to repeat something.

12. When talking with a person who has a vision impairment, describe things specifically. Avoid generalities such as "over there" or "down here." One effective technique when at a fixed setting such as an office, is to describe things in terms of a clock face. For example, you might say that the tape recorder is at 3 or the Braille machine is at 9.

One thought should be kept in mind: When you make a mistake, apologize for your error and return to being natural. There is no reason to gush over your faux pas or burden yourself with excess guilt.

A Final Note

Although historic misconceptions have evolved, today's reality is that persons with disabilities are now recognized as an intrinsic part of society. Other groups, such as minorities and women, have developed new words and phrases which are now preferred, because the language mirrors our attitudes.

Impairments or disabilities are physiological. They become handicaps when accommodations, including those of the mind are not made. Attitudinal barriers can create and perpetuate other barriers in the physical environment as well as in routine interpersonal interactions.

The next several chapters cover particular aspects of persons interacting in society. Mannerism and language can be helpful in attaining positive interactions on substantive matters. Irrational, unfounded fears are illegal as well as counterproductive. Utilizing the right words and techniques will facilitate achieving solutions and enhance the benefits to all.

Chapter 2

EMPLOYMENT

Introduction

One day one of my children saw a "Hire the Handicapped" poster in a window and asked what it meant. In his youthful innocence the question came out, "Is that sign for real? Shouldn't people who get hired not be handicapped—I mean able to do the job?"

Before I could explain that the poster was intended to make people realize that people with disabilities could do the job, a friend interjected, "It's really for employers to know they aren't handicapping themselves by hiring a person with a disability."

Another friend added that if everyone hired a person with a disability during that week there would be no need for laws prohibiting discrimination against persons with disabilities in employment.

All of us, including my child, were right. There have been many "Hire the Handicapped" weeks and months. Many persons with disabilities can do the job. Employers are not limiting themselves by hiring and promoting qualified persons with disabilities.

Unfortunately, while there are laws prohibiting discrimination against qualified disabled persons, there are problems in the employment processes. But there is a wide range of practical solutions available.

This chapter provides overviews of federal and state laws prohibiting discrimination in employment. Practical materials, including a model reasonable accommodations policy, outreach recruiting hints, as well as certain questions which may and may not be asked when interviewing and on job applications, are set forth. The objective is to provide a practical perspective on what it means to "hire the handicapped."

Federal Law

There are now three major statutes which provide coverage for persons with disabilities. These laws are the Americans with Disabilities Act, the Rehabilitation Act and the Vietnam Era Veterans Readjustment Act.

The Americans with Disabilities Act (ADA), enacted in the summer of 1990, is the centerpiece of the legislation providing a comprehensive set of rights and responsibilities related to equal employment opportunity for persons with disabilities and their employers. In a nutshell, when fully implemented, ADA will afford persons with disabilities protected status under federal employment law as has been accorded minorities since enactment of the Civil Rights Act of 1964. The employment provisions of ADA draw heavily on concepts established since 1973 under the Rehabilitation Act, discussed *infra*, as well as the Civil Rights Act of 1964.

The Americans with Disabilities Act is an equal opportunity (not guarantee of employment) law. The ADA affords qualified individuals with a disability protection from discrimination by employers in all aspects of the employment relationship — hiring, discharge, compensation, advancement, training, benefits, insurance, or other terms, conditions, and privileges of employment. The definitions of terms such as employer and labor organizations are based on the definitions of those terms in Title VII of the Civil Rights Act of 1964. These are broad terms, encompassing most private and public employers, including traditional private sector businesses, state and local governments, as well as unions.

Under the ADA, Title I, a "qualified individual with a disability" is an individual with a disability who, with or without reasonable accommodation, can perform the essential functions of the job that the individual holds or desires. The term individual with a disability includes a person with a physical or mental impairment that substantially limits one or more of the major life activities of the individual, who has a record of such an impairment or a person who is regarded as having such an impairment. ADA defines disability in terms of functionality—an impairment, physical or mental, that limits major life activities. ADA also covers persons who are perceived as disabled. This ADA definition is derived from the Rehabilitation Act.

Crucially, ADA does not enumerate all disabilities covered. The definition embraces persons with many diverse disabilities. It includes those individuals whose impairment may affect their mobility, hearing, or vision, as well as persons with neurological disabilities, or speech impairments, or specific learning disabilities. It includes persons with AIDS (or those who are HIV positive), as well as persons with alcoholism and former drug users who have completed or are participating in a drug rehabilitation program. Persons wrongfully perceived as illegal drug users, who, in fact, are not such users, are also covered. Current illegal drug users are not covered when the employer acts on the basis of the illegal drug use. Homosexuality, bisexuality, and other specified conditions, such as transvestism, are not considered disabilities under ADA. A person who associates with an individual with a disability may not be discriminated against because of the other person's known disability.

ADA does not cover employees of tax-exempt private clubs, Indian tribes, or the federal government. The Rehabilitation Act covers federal government employment. ADA allows religious entities to give preference in employment to individuals of the particular religion as well as to require all employees to conform to the religious tenets of the organizations.

ADA is markedly more inclusive than the Rehabilitation Act (Rehab Act) and Vietnam Veterans Readjustment Act (VVRA), since the employment nondiscrimination mandate applies even if there is no direct nexus between the employer and federal government through a grant of federal financial assistance or a federal contract. The Rehab Act and VVRA apply only if the employer receives federal money or other aid.

Critically, the ADA Title I phases in coverage. The employment provisions are effective two years after enactment, i.e., July 26, 1992. For the next two years, i.e., two years after the effective date of enactment, only employers with 25 or more employees are covered. As of July 26, 1994, ADA coverage expands to employers with 15 or more employees. Employers with fewer than 15 employees are not covered by ADA (though such employers may well be covered by state laws which are presently applicable). Federal regulations in the employment area must be issued by July 26, 1991, a year after ADA was enacted.

The ADA mandate not to discriminate in employment at section 102 of the statute includes prohibiting a covered employer from:

1. limiting, classifying, or segregating an applicant or employee in a manner that adversely affects that person because of their disability.

2. participating in a contract or other arrangement that has the effect of discriminating on the basis of disability against an applicant or employee.

3. utilizing standards, criteria, or methods which have the effect of discriminating or perpetuating discrimination.

4. excluding or denying job benefits to a qualified person because of the known disability of person with whom the qualified person is related or associated.

5. selecting or administering employment related tests that screen out disabled persons.

6. using qualification standards or tests that screen out persons with disabilities.

Other prohibitions are also important and most sensitive. They relate to making reasonable accommodations, medical examinations, and disability related inquiries.

Employers must make reasonable accommodations to the known limitations of the qualified individual with a disability unless the accommodation would be an undue hardship. Decisions as to reasonable accommodations are best approached on an individualized, case-by-case basis, though there are general principles to be followed.

Reasonable accommodation is a concept which arose in the implementation of the Rehabilitation Act, and includes job restructuring, modifying work schedules, providing auxiliary aids and services, removing architectural barriers, and revising or adjusting examinations, training materials or policies.

To determine whether an accommodation would pose an undue hardship, i.e., an administrative or financial burden, several factors related to the accommodation, the employer, in general, and the specific employment site may be considered. These include the nature and cost of the accommodation; the size of the business in terms of the numbers and types of employees, facilities, and financial resources; the impact of the accommodation on the operation of the facility, and the type of operation(s) and separateness, administrative, or fiscal relationship of the facility or facilities in question.

Bear in mind that as Title IV of ADA is implemented by telecommunications carriers, auxiliary services for hearing and speech impaired persons will be more readily available. Title IV requires telecommunication relay services to be provided by telephone service providers no later than July 26, 1993, three years after ADA became effective. The Federal Communications Commission, which enforces these provisions, is to issue regulations by July 26, 1991. This Title should also lead to easier compliance with the reasonable accommodation mandate of the Rehabilitation Act as well as the public accommodations provisions in Title III of ADA (discussed at greater length in Chapter 3).

Under ADA employers may still apply job-related tests and selection criteria, consistent with business needs. Employers are permitted to make pre-employment inquiries into the ability of an applicant to perform job related functions — as opposed to inquiring directly whether an applicant has a disability or the nature/severity of such disability.

Under ADA an employer's written job or position description prepared before interviewing or advertising for a position is expressly evidence of the essential job functions. It is also a tool for management to review what employees are really required to do to succeed in their work.

Under ADA, employers are not to conduct or require a medical examination or make inquiry to determine whether an applicant or employee has a disability or to determine the nature/severity of the disability unless the examination/inquiry is job-related and consistent with business necessity.

Employers are permitted to require employees take medical examinations provided it is after employment has been offered, all employees of that category take examinations, the results are kept confidential and used only in accordance with ADA. While ADA expressly provides a pre-employment physical is acceptable if given to "all entering employees," all committee reports with the law indicate this phrase means only all employees of a particular category, not all employees, e.g., to an applicant for a mechanic's position if all entering mechanics (not the accountants, personnel staff, purchasers, etc.) were also subject to examination. Confidentiality of medical records (except as needed for medical and supervisory personnel and government investigations) is required.

While persons with Acquired Immune Deficiency Syndrome (AIDS), HIV positive and rehabilitated drug users are covered, current illegal drug users are not protected when the employer acts on that basis. Also, employers need not hire or retain an individual who has a currently contagious disease or infection or other condition, which even with reasonable accommodation, poses a direct threat to the health or safety of others in the workplace. An individual who because of the currently contagious disease or infection or other health condition is unable to do the job is not protected by ADA. By January 26, 1991, six months after enactment of ADA, the Secretary of the United States Department of Health and Human Services was to publish a list of infectious and communicable diseases which can be transmitted through food handling. Annual updates of the list are required. Employers may reassign employees with conditions on the list and who cannot otherwise be reasonably accommodated to non-food handling positions without violating ADA. (For additional materials on AIDS and employment see Appendix III.)

It is permissible for management to prohibit employees from using or being under the influence of alcohol and illegal drugs at the workplace. All employees can be held to conform to the federal Drug-Free Workplace Act of 1988. Employers may also require adherence to federal alcohol and drug regulations related to employment established by the Department of Defense, Nuclear Regulatory Commission, and the Department of Transportation. A drug user or alcoholic may be held to the same qualifications standards for employment and job performance/behavior to which nonaffected persons are held, even if the individual's unsatisfactory performance/behavior is related to the alcohol or drug use. ADA does not make corporate wellness programs illegal.

Employers and labor organizations must post notices to employees, applicants, and members describing the ADA. Also an employer cannot contract or participate in any other arrangement which subjects its qualified disabled applicants or employees to discrimination. These provisions parallel provisions in the Civil Rights Act of 1964. These provisions promote greater awareness of ADA and prohibit employers from doing indirectly what ADA prohibits them from doing directly.

Also, like the Civil Rights Act, qualified applicants and employees with disabilities are protected by ADA if their actions are based on their unwillingness to engage in futile gestures.

Under ADA Title I, individuals are given the right to complain to the United States Equal Employment Opportunity Commission (EEOC) and go to court, obtain specific relief, such as the job or promotion, as well as recover back pay. EEOC is required to issue its implementing regulations by July 26, 1991, one year after the effective date of the ADA. Courts can enjoin intentional discrimination. Attorney's fees are recoverable in both the administrative proceedings as well as in court cases. Also under Title I, the United States Department of Justice, led by the Attorney General, has authority to pursue the more widespread violations by state and local governments, the "pattern and practice" violations.

Employment by all state and local governments is also subject to Title II of ADA, which mandates nondiscrimination in all services, programs and activities of such entities. The Attorney General must issue regulations by July 26, 1991, one year after ADA was enacted, to carry out this Title. Title II becomes effective on January 26, 1992, eighteen months after ADA became law. Individuals have the right to go to court and recover back pay, as well as attorney's fees. Unlike Title I, which phases in coverage and exempts the very small employer, i.e., one with less than 15 employees, Title II covers all state and local governments (no exemptions) and does not stagger in the effective dates of coverage. ADA expressly requires coordination between the federal agencies, which should lead to similar substantive requirements under Titles I and II.

Under the civil rights bill considered late in 1990, individuals proving discrimination under ADA could, after a jury trial, be awarded compensatory damages to redress the consequences of the proven employment discrimination. In egregious cases, punitive damages, up to $100,000 could be recovered. While the 1990 bill was not enacted, similar legislation will be considered in 1991 and 1992 by the 102nd Congress.

The ADA is based on principles previously articulated as the requirements of the Rehabilitation Act. Enactment of ADA included with it several amendments to the Rehabilitation Act, such as to the definition of handicapped individual, so that the ADA and the Rehabilitation Act should be interpreted and applied consistently. It is on the Rehabilitation Act that we now focus.

Title V of the Rehabilitation Act contains three key employment mandates. These provisions apply to recipients of federal financial assistance, federal contractors, and the federal government, sections 504, 503, and 501, respectively.

Most important is section 504 which prohibits discrimination by recipients of federal aid. While it was controverted at one time, it is now well established that under the Rehabilitation Act discrimination in employment against qualified individuals with disabilities is prohibited under a federal grant. This is true even if the main purpose of the grant is not for employment but is to provide services, such as library or transit.

As a result of the Civil Rights Restoration Act (CRRA) of 1988, it is now law that the nondiscrimination mandate of section 504 applies not only to those specific programs receiving federal aid but generally to all of a recipient's programs. This is the case if the recipient is a department, agency, special purpose district, or other instrumentality of a state or local government (if the state or local government entity distributes the aid to another department or agency, then both entities are covered), a college, university, or public system of higher education, an elementary or secondary school system.

Under the Civil Rights Restoration Act with respect to private corporations, if the federal aid is extended to the corporation as a whole, classically the aid to the Chrysler Corporation to keep the company from going bankrupt, the entire corporation is covered. If the corporation provides a public service, such as social services, education or housing, parks or recreation, then the entire corporation also is covered. However, if the corporation is not in such a public service business and the federal aid is extended to only one plant or a geographically separate facility, only that plant is covered. Two facilities that are part of a complex or that are proximate to each other in the same city would not be considered geographically separate. In the case of some hybrid partnership between a college and a corporation or the government and the private sector or other entities established by two or more of the previously discussed types of recipients, then the entire entity is covered if it receives any federal assistance. By adopting the Civil Rights Restoration Act, Congress legislatively reversed *Grove City v. Bell*, 465 U.S.555 (1984), which had limited the application of federal civil rights mandates to the specific programs receiving the assistance (as opposed to all activities and programs of the recipient).

Section 504 of the Rehabilitation Act is implemented by regulations issued by the federal agencies. Typically, those agency regulations will prohibit an employer from discriminating in recruiting, advertising, and processing of applications, hiring, tenure, promotion, transfer, layoffs, terminations, rehiring, rates of pay or any other form of compensation, job assignments, position descriptions, seniority, lines of progression, leave (annual, sick or other), fringe benefits, training and related activities, employer sponsored activities including social and recreational programs, or any other term, condition, or privilege of employment.

In a nutshell, qualified handicapped persons must be afforded the same opportunities afforded their non-disabled colleagues in all phases of employment.

It is important to note that for purposes of section 504 and section 503 as they relate to employment, the key definition, that of handicapped individual, is an individual who has a physical or mental impairment which substantially limits one or more of such person's major life activities, has a record of such an impairment, or is regarded as having such an impairment.

A key and emotional issue has been whether persons with Acquired Immune Deficiency Syndrome (AIDS) are within the definition of "handicapped individual" under the Rehabilitation Act. The United States Supreme Court in the landmark case *School Board of Nassau County, Florida v. Arline*, 480 U.S. 273 (1987), did NOT decide that a person with AIDS or an AIDS carrier was a handicapped individual under federal law. It stated that the mere fear of contagion from an underlying physical illness could not be a basis for terminating an individual, in the particular case, an individual who had tuberculosis. The United States Supreme Court left open the AIDS questions. However, lower federal courts, as well as the federal Departments of Justice, Health and Human Services, and Labor, have considered AIDS a handicapping condition under the Rehabilitation Act.

The Civil Rights Restoration Act codified this by making clear that, for purposes of sections 503 and 504 of the Rehabilitation Act, as related to employment, a person who had a currently contagious disease or infection, and who, by reason of such disease or infection, would constitute a direct threat to the health or safety of other individuals, or who by reason of the currently contagious disease or infection was unable to do the job, was not covered by the law.

Also not covered under the Rehabilitation Act, are those individuals who are alcohol or drug abusers where the current use of alcohol or drugs prevents the individual from performing the duties of the job in question or would endanger others. Also excluded are individuals whose employment would constitute a direct threat to property or safety of others because of such current alcohol or drug use. When ADA was adopted, the Rehab Act was amended to contain similarly identical provisions related to drug users. Current illegal drug users are excluded from the Rehab Act when the employer acts on the basis of such drug use. Former drug users or persons who have completed a drug rehabilitation program are covered, as are persons perceived as drug users who are not drug users.

It is critical to note that many persons with disabilities, as well as many persons who are not within the traditional definition of "handicapped individual" take medications and may still be considered qualified for employment. Taking medication per se is not enough to exclude a person from protection under the Rehabilitation Act or ADA.

Both the Rehab Act and ADA are in addition to, not instead of, other federal, state, and local laws prohibiting drugs and alcohol in the workplace.

Regulations of the federal agencies implementing section 504 make clear that a qualified handicapped individual is one who, with (or without) reasonable accommodation, can perform the essential functions of the job in question.

The obligation of employers is thus two-fold: to have an awareness of the essential functions of the job and to provide reasonable accommodations when needed.

What are the essential functions of the job? Answer: an analysis of the position, its tasks and their frequency, requisite skills and training, job environment, and whatever else may be required for the job to be done, including travel or other bona fide occupational elements.

The key in understanding the essential functions of the job is to look at the job realistically—to know what a person must do to accomplish the purpose of the position.

The concept of reasonable accommodation under section 504 of the Rehabilitation Act is one of adapting the work environment to the known physical or mental limitations of disabled applicants and employees. This must be done unless the recipient can show that this would be an undue hardship on the operation of its program. This entails ascertaining the size, in terms of employees, facilities and budget, nature and structure of the work force, as well as nature and extent of the cost the needed accommodation. Safety becomes a factor, too.

Reasonable accommodation embraces ideas which many firms already utilize, even without calling it that. For example, reasonable accommodation may include making facilities more accessible, using flexible working hours, providing assistive devices or equipment, providing readers or interpreters, modifying work sites, or even modifying the job itself by reassigning duties amongst several positions.

Many organizations are already on "flex time" and are utilizing technologically advanced equipment that can be modified for use by employees with disabilities. The accessible workplace, while ostensibly for the employee with a disability, is accessible to all employees. In new structures accessibility codes (see Chapter 3) mandate access.

Over the years the question of what is a reasonable accommodation has been one of the most litigious. It represents the question of how far a recipient must go to satisfy the nondiscrimination mandate of the federal statute.

In one early case, the United States Supreme Court held that a recipient of federal financial assistance need not make substantial or major adjustments and modifications to its programs to allow a handicapped person to participate in it if the person could not reasonably be expected to perform the tasks that a typical graduate of its program would be required to perform. An "otherwise qualified individual with a handicap" is one who is able to meet the program requirements including physical qualifications, despite his handicap, *Davis v. Southeastern Community College*, 442 U.S. 397 (1979).

More recently the Supreme Court has made clear that meaningful access must be provided to programs. However, the Court reiterated that substantial changes or modifications in a program or those which would constitute a fundamental alteration in the nature of the program were not required, *Alexander v. Choate*, 469 U.S. 287 (1985).

Cases involving reasonable accommodation have proliferated. Court rulings make clear that an employer must have objective evidence to support its position. Mere speculation is not enough. Also, an employer must consider the alternative positions that may be available to accommodate qualified persons with disabilities.

In my practice, I have encountered employers who simply want to know what they should do. A basic, practical hint: AFTER the employment/hiring/promotion/transfer/etc. decision has been made, and the person found otherwise qualified, ask the employee or applicant what accommodation he thinks would suit him. It has never ceased to amaze me how we know our own limits and needs.

I recall working in the San Francisco area with a colleague who had the use of only one hand and whose fingers on the other hand were of limited use. He told his employer that what he needed at his desk was to have strings attached to the handles of the drawers. My friend had enough use of his "handicapped" hand to be able to pull on a piece of string to open the desk drawer. There was no need for an electronic mechanism. Total cost of the accommodation: 20¢.

In reviewing accommodations, employers may wish to establish a management committee, as set forth in the model reasonable accommodations policy later in this chapter. That ensures input from the diverse elements of the firm, as well as an institutional memory on which to draw to address future situations.

In analyzing an accommodation, consider the following questions to determine if the accommodation is reasonable:

1. Are the requirements for all positions for which the person with a disability may be hired/transferred/promoted, etc. legitimate, necessary, equitable, and reasonable?
2. Are the requirements uniformly applied to all applicants and employees?
3. What functions can the person with a disability perform?
4. What are the specific accommodations necessary to enable the person with a disability to perform the tasks and how do they impact on the organization in terms of business necessity or undue hardship?

The answers to those questions must be documented on the basis of factual evidence.

Recipients of assistance must give notice that they do not discriminate against qualified handicapped persons, just as they give notice that they do not discriminate against any other protected class, such as minorities and women.

There are two other areas under section 504 of the Rehabilitation Act, pre-employment medical examinations and pre-employment medical inquiries, that are somewhat unique to discrimination against handicapped persons. The rules in these areas underscore the need for prospective employers to follow a basic tenet applicable to all prospective employment situations: limit pre-employment inquiries to the applicant's ability to perform job related functions.

In the first area, that of pre-employment medical examinations, such examinations are allowed provided that the medical examinations follow conditional offers of employment, all entering employees in the particular category of work are subjected to such examinations regardless of whether they are handicapped; the results of the examinations are used only in accordance with regulations issued under section 504; and the information is collected and maintained in separate forms that are accorded confidentiality as medical records. This is the same under ADA.

The second unique area is that of pre-employment medical inquiries. Generally, these are not allowed. However, these inquiries may be made where affirmative action is being taken under section 503 by a federal contractor or the recipient is taking government-ordered remedial action to overcome the effects of past discrimination. Pre-employment medical inquiries may also be made where a recipient is taking voluntary action to overcome the effects of conditions that resulted in limited participation in past programs and activities.

Where such inquiry is allowed, the employer must make clear the basis for the inquiry, that the information requested is sought on a voluntary basis, there will be no recriminations for failing to provide the information, the information will be collected and kept confidential as medical records, and used only in accordance with the applicable regulations.

The net result is not to prohibit pre-employment medical inquiries, but rather is to make clear that those inquiries not related to the performance of job related functions cannot be the basis of a hiring decision and to place stringent limits on the use of any information collected. It is an acceptable business practice to make an employee undergo a physical examination where the physical will check or reveal the ability of the employee to perform bona fide occupational qualifications. As under ADA, the examination must be given to all in the particular job category.

In the *School Board of Nassau County, Florida v. Arline* 480 U.S.273 (1987), decision the United States Supreme Court provided guidance on the use of medical information in making reasonable accommodations for an employee. The Court decided that an individual, otherwise qualified, who had tuberculosis, could not be terminated simply because of the contagiousness of the condition and set forth the medical information to be gathered in order to make a medically and programmatically sound decision (as opposed to a decision predicated on fear, ignorance, and without documentation) whether a contagious individual was "otherwise qualified":

1. Nature of the risk, i.e., how the disease is transmitted.
2. Duration of the risk, i.e., how long the carrier is infectious.
3. Severity of the risk, i.e., what is the potential harm to third parties, such as co-workers.
4. Probabilities the disease will be transmitted and will cause varying degrees of harm.

With this information, the employer must then apply the established reasonable accommodations criteria. Courts, in reviewing these decisions, will defer to reasonable medical judgments but will require documentation.

On a related note, the United States Department of Labor, Occupational Safety and Health Administration is considering issuing rules to regulate hospital and other health care workers who are exposed to AIDS and other blood-borne diseases. These would be the first workplace requirements related to AIDS imposed by the federal government, though the Centers for Disease Control have issued several often used recommendations.

Individuals who believe their rights under section 504 of the Rehabilitation Act have been violated may seek redress through the federal agency providing the financial assistance or they may proceed to file suit in federal court. Attorney's fees are recoverable in such actions.

The remedies for the aggrieved person with disabilities include all the traditional remedies of equal employment cases — back pay, seniority, and related benefits. The federal agency providing the benefits can terminate the assistance or find the aid recipient ineligible for future benefits if they are found to have discriminated. This was not affected by the Civil Rights Restoration Act or ADA.

Section 503 of the Rehabilitation Act and Vietnam Era Veterans Readjustment Assistance Act are statutes requiring affirmative action in hiring and promoting persons with disabilities. The definition of handicapped person in section 503 is that which has been previously discussed under section 504. Under the Vietnam Era provisions, the veteran must have a 30 percent disability rating or have been discharged or released because of a service related disability.

Both statutes are affirmative action statutes in all phases and employment practices of a federal contractor or subcontractor, including hiring, promoting, training, recruiting, apprentice programs, layoffs, etc.

The statute applies where the amount of the contract or subcontract is $2,500 or more. Larger employers, i.e., those with a contract of $50,000 or more or 50 or more employees, must develop an affirmative action plan for handicapped employees. This is the same type of program other protected classes have applicable to them in terms of the policy and substantive requirements.

Mental and physical qualifications must be job related, consistent with business necessity and safe performance, so as not to screen out otherwise qualified handicapped persons.

There is a requirement that the job site be accessible for the qualified handicapped person, though no technical standard is

specified. Recipients and other organizations would do well to
adhere to the access standards under federal grants they have,
the technical standard under their state code, or the Uniform
Federal Accessibility Standard. (Previously the American National Standard Institute standard for access, A117.1, was applied.) Those standards are discussed at greater length in the
next chapter. Reasonable accommodation to the known disabling
conditions is required. This obligation is limited by considerations of business necessity, costs, and safety.

Both the Vietnam Era Readjustment Assistance Act and section 503 of the Rehabilitation Act are enforceable by the United
States Department of Labor. It is now settled that the statutes do
not create private causes of action on which alleged victims may
proceed to court directly. The Department of Labor, Office of
Federal Contract Compliance, is responsible for enforcing both
statutes. Courts have generally deferred to the judgment and
discretion of the Department of Labor in enforcing these two
laws.

Two other statutes worthy of mention are section 501 of the
Rehabilitation Act and the Architectural Barriers Act. Section
501 requires affirmative action and nondiscrimination by the
federal government. Federal employees are also covered by
amendments to section 504 of the Rehabilitation Act applying it
to the activities of the federal government itself. The practical
result is that federal agencies must not discriminate and must
have affirmative action plans for hiring qualified handicapped
employees. The employment practices covered are the same. As
the federal government strives to be the model employer, federal
agencies are required to develop affirmative action program
plans for the hiring, placement, and advancement of handicapped individuals.

Federal employees have an administrative remedy in the form
of the Equal Employment Opportunity Commission. Depending
upon how the case arises, the federal employee may also be able
to seek redress through the Merit Systems Protection Board,
another administrative agency. Federal employees may file suit

in federal court as well. In these forums attorney's fees are available.

The Architectural Barriers Act, discussed at greater length in Chapter 3, is employment related because it requires compliance with accessibility standards in buildings subject to access standards in which persons with disabilities may be employed. However, the remedy under that Act would be to make the building or facility within it accessible. It would not necessarily result in the aggrieved person obtaining a job.

In summary, there are now widely applicable federal laws prohibiting discrimination against qualified individuals with disabilities or handicaps. As a result of the Americans with Disabilities Act and Civil Rights Restoration Act, federal equal employment mandates are no longer limited to the specific federal programs receiving financial aid or having a government contract. Federal laws reach most private sector employer-employee relationships. In this respect, the federal laws have come closer to the state and local laws to which we now turn.

State And Local Laws

State and local laws are critically important. While the broadest federal anti-employment discrimination law, the Americans with Disabilities Act, will be phasing into applicability through 1994, these laws are in effect now and cover traditional employment relations, whether or not there is any federal financial nexus by means of grant or contract. Also, the state laws tend to cover more of the smaller employers than the ADA, as the state law exemptions from coverage (noted in Appendix I) are often lower than the fifteen employees in ADA.

State laws are very pervasive since they usually do not require state involvement in the form of a grant or contract to be applicable. State laws can apply to the everyday employment situations at a hospital, college, corporation, or non-profit organization. Also, state laws may provide for the award of damages and attorney's fees to victims of discrimination.

It is also interesting to observe that at the state level employment discrimination laws, unlike the federal law, may also have a criminal sanction. "White Cane" laws, adopted in almost every state, make it a criminal misdemeanor to discriminate in employment against blind and other handicapped persons.

In approaching state laws affecting employment practices and handicapped persons, it is important to note that those laws are commonly found in state civil rights, human rights, or anti-discrimination statutes. State employment discrimination laws affecting minorities, women, and persons with disabilities are commonly grouped together. States commonly have pre-employment guidelines explicitly indicating in each of these areas the types of inquiries which are acceptable as well as those which are prohibited.

As a practical matter, in every state the Governor's office will have access to the law affecting employment and persons with disabilities. There is a state committee, frequently called the Governor's Committee on Employment of People with Disabilities, which can provide the law upon request. These, too, are noted in Appendix I.

At the local level, there may be county or municipal committees or commissions on disabled individuals. These are also potential sources to obtain copies of the local law as well as state laws.

The threshold questions to ask are who is covered and what activities are covered.

The "Who is covered?" is really two questions: Which individuals are protected by the law? and Which employers must comply with the law?

State laws vary widely and thus there is no uniform answer to these questions. There are certain trends and categories.

Many states and local jurisdictions have come to accept and adopt the federal definition found in section 504. That means they provide protection for persons with physical or mental impairments that substantially limit one or more of the person's major life activities, who have a record of such an impairment, or who are regarded as having such an impairment. This is the law in states such as Illinois and Maryland.

Note carefully, not all states follow the federal law with respect to alcohol and drug abusers. This is a crucial distinction since alcoholism and drug abuse are two of the top problems in employment.

Several states have laws but do not define "disabled" or "handicapped" in the statute. In those states you need to check the regulations of the state agency implementing the law for their definition of "disabled" or "handicapped" as it will elaborate on the meaning of the statute by indicating the nature of the disabilities, i.e., physical, mental, or other, to which it applies.

In analyzing a state law for coverage of "handicapped" or "disabled" persons, check whether persons with physical or mental impairments are covered as well as whether persons perceived or regarded as disabled or handicapped are protected. State laws also commonly enumerate who is covered, e.g., persons who are blind, deaf, mobility impaired. Not all states cover persons with mental impairments, e.g., Arizona. At the other end of the spectrum, the Massachusetts law protects persons who are recovered from a disability. California expressly protects cancer patients, who reasonably would be considered under other laws as persons perceived or regarded as having a disability.

In several states, as noted in Appendix I, there are express provisions related to Acquired Immunity Deficiency Syndrome (AIDS). Those include Iowa, Missouri, Oregon, Florida, and Washington. In many other states, such as New York, Michigan, and the District of Columbia, public officials issued strong pronouncements stating that AIDS was considered a handicapping condition covered by the human rights law prohibiting discrimination against persons with disabilities. In the 1980s state administrative agencies and state courts ruled persons with AIDS were within the definition of handicapped persons under state laws. Also, many states, such as Illinois, Indiana, and West Virginia, adopted testing and confidentiality laws.

The other side of the "who" issue is who is obligated not to discriminate and who must take appropriate action. Most commonly, government agencies, private employers, labor unions or organizations, and employment agencies are required to comply with the law. Also covered by mnay state laws are those employers receiving state funds or providing a state supported program or activity or a training and apprenticeship program.

Commonly, states make exceptions for the small employers. The popular vision of the "Mom and Pop" store now is large enough to encompass employers with a set small number of helping hands, often 15 or less. See Appendix I. This needs to be checked in each state.

State laws prohibiting discrimination against handicapped persons afford them the same protections as other classes protected in their jurisdiction. This means the entire gamut of employment practices—from advertising and application to seniority and termination—are subject to scrutiny. The thrust in each of these phases of employment is to make reasonable accommodation, discussed at length in the federal law, as well as not to discriminate.

State laws may contain exceptions expressly written into them. As noted previously, the definition of "handicapped" may in reality be an exception by excluding different types who are not within it. Also, state laws may expressly allow an exception for a bona fide occupational qualification. This traditional exception from the requirements of equal employment law is another approach to ensure what the federal law considers a "qualified" individual with a disability. Some states may approach the problem by noting that there is no discrimination where the person's disability precludes them from performing the work.

State laws, unlike the federal statute, may point expressly to the need for professional documentation, normally from a physician. That is the case in Georgia, Maine, and Nebraska. The statute prescribes the objective evidence that an employer should have in formulating the decision as to whether the particular individual can be accommodated without an undue or burdensome hardship. Industrial engineering advice may also be of value here. Medical information is especially critical where there may be a serious health issue.

No review of state laws would be complete without a few brief pointers about enforcement. An allegedly aggrieved employee, present or former, or applicant, can file a formal complaint either with the state fair employment practices (i.e., civil or human rights) agency which administers the law, or directly in state court. Such is the practice in Maine, Texas and New York. In other jurisdictions (Maryland, Ohio, and Kansas) the law is enforced exclusively by the civil or human rights commissions through an investigative process that culminates in a public administrative due process hearing. In all states, the criminal sanction of the "White Cane" law is for the state attorney general, not the aggrieved individual, to enforce in the courts.

County and municipal ordinances follow the same patterns. Local human relations commissions can enforce the county ordinances. It is to be noted that in certain states incorporated cities do not fall under county ordinances and alleged violations within them must be addressed under the city law or the state law.

The remedies under the state and local laws are varied. They can include injunctive relief, back pay, and damages. In a few jurisdictions, attorney's fees are also available to a successful litigant.

State and local laws are crucial. They complement and expand upon federal law. The questions really are how to avoid problems and do what must be done. The following sections address those concerns. Some positive incentives are noted. A model reasonable accommodations policy is set forth. Recruiting outreach techniques are noted as are germane questions that can be asked and which must be answered truthfully. Questions which are generally not to be used are also noted.

Incentives

Many persons with disabilities want to work. Studies have shown that persons with disabilities do not experience undue or excessive absenteeism. In fact, their attendance record is quite good, leading to greater stability in the workforce. A study of federal contractors found that making reasonable accommodations did not entail much cost. Experience also teaches that, with a willing employee, it is more cost effective for management to retrain an injured employee for a new position, rather than have the employee retire on disability. All of this takes on increasing practical importance as we move towards the realities of Workforce 2000.

In addition there are tax incentives for hiring and accommodating persons with disabilities. The Targeted Job Tax Credit gives employers a credit of 40 percent of the first year wages (up to $6,000 per employee) of "disadvantaged" people, a category which includes persons with disabilities who have been referred to an employer from the state vocational rehabilitation program or the United States Department of Veterans Affairs. There is also a deduction for businesses that remove architectural, transportation and communication barriers. The 1990 tax law authorizes credits of up to $5,000 per year for small businesses (30 or fewer employees and less and $1 million gross sales) operating places of public accommodation (see Chapter 3), providing auxiliary aids and services to their employees with disabilities. As part of this legislation, the barrier removal deduction, fixed at $35,000 since 1986 was reduced to a maximum of $15,000, commencing in 1991 when both measures became effective.

Reasonable Accommodations: A Sample Policy*

NOTE: This is only a sample. Readers are cautioned to check federal, state, and local laws and regulations. This is a model which may be used as a point of departure. An employer does not have to hire, promote, etc. an employee who cannot, even with reasonable accommodation, perform the essentials of the job.

I. Statement of Purpose

It is the policy of this organization to provide reasonable accommodations for qualified individuals with disabilities who are employees or applicants for employment. This organization will adhere to all applicable federal, state, and local laws, regulations, and guidelines with respect to providing reasonable accommodations as required to afford equal employment opportunity to qualified individuals with disabilities. Reasonable accommodations shall be provided in a timely and cost-effective manner.

II. Definitions

Individual with a Disability. Any person who has or has acquired a physical or mental impairment, has a record of such impairment, or is regarded as having such an impairment, which limits one or more major life activities, such as self care, performing manual tasks, seeing, hearing, speaking, breathing, and working on a temporary or permanent basis.

Physical or mental impairment. Any physiological disorder, disfigurement, or anatomical loss or limitation, or any mental or psychological disorder acquired as a result of illness, accident or birth.

---

*   Reprinted from the *Handicapped Requirements Handbook*, with permission of Thompson Publishing Group, Washington, D.C., in which the original materials upon which this is based, were printed.

Qualified individual with a disability. An individual with a disability whose experience, education, and/or training enable the person, with reasonable accommodation, to perform the essential functions of the job.

Reasonable Accommodation. That effort made to make adjustments for the impairment of an employee or applicant by structuring the job or work environment in a manner that will enable the disabled individual to perform the essential functions of the job. Reasonable accommodation includes, but is not limited to, modifying written examinations, making facilities accessible, adjusting work schedules, restructuring jobs, providing assistive devices or equipment, providing readers or interpreters, and modifying work sites.

Reasonable Accommodations Committee. Although not expressly required in regulations, this committee is established to review and monitor provision of reasonable accommodations to employees and applicants in an effective and equitable manner. The committee shall be composed of representatives from the Personnel Department, Equal Employment Opportunity Department, and Management Division. Medical and facility management units shall also designate a member to serve in an ex-officio or advisory capacity.

III. Practices

1. Managers and supervisors shall prepare an analysis of jobs within their units, which shall include defining the essential functional elements or tasks as well as the environment in which such activities occur. Such documentation shall be developed with the assistance of the personnel director and shall be reviewed periodically. Documents prepared or utilized for this purpose may be used for other personnel actions.

2. In considering an individual with a disability for employment or for promotion or in any other personnel action, the existence of their disabling condition should not adversely affect a personnel decision. Employment opportunities shall not be

denied to anyone because of the need to make reasonable accommodations to the individual's disabling condition.

3. In considering a person with a disability, it is appropriate to determine the ability of the person to perform the essential functions of the job with reasonable accommodation. A request for medical verification of the disability of the person requesting the accommodation may be appropriate. It is also appropriate to consider whether the providing of the accommodation would be an undue hardship.

4. Immediate supervisors shall have the authority to make reasonable accommodations for applicants or employees which do not exceed $____ (a given dollar amount) or are totally within the work station or work site of the individual with a disability.

5. The committee shall meet periodically, at least quarterly, to review all reasonable accommodations made by immediate supervisors. It shall meet as needed to review other proposed or requested accommodations which cannot be addressed by immediate supervisors. The committee shall review all accommodations possibly involving an undue hardship for the company and, promptly obtain all information necessary to review such proposed accommodations and alternatives thereto. The committee shall consult with the individual who is disabled and immediate supervisor involved where necessary. It shall act in a timely manner that will enable personnel actions to proceed to their regular course. The committee shall forward an annual report of its activities to all unit managers.

6. If the employee wishes to challenge the decision of the committee, the employee shall have access to existing grievance procedure.

7. The employee and his/her supervisor should periodically monitor the effectiveness of the accommodation.

8. Individuals with disabilities shall be afforded the opportunity to provide reasonable accommodations for themselves where for the business to do so would impose an undue hardship on the operation of the business. The disabled individual shall not be afforded the opportunity to make accommodations which

affect a temporary or permanent change to the facilities of this institution or which involve restructuring of the job in question without the written consent of all individuals and departments involved.

IV. Implementation

This policy shall be implemented as part of the personnel policy of this institution and shall be reviewed regularly as part of the administration of such practices.

Recruiting Techniques

"How do I find one?" a friend implored after hearing the standard lecture on hiring a qualified person with a disability.

Translating good intentions into a live worker can be difficult at times. Here are some practical suggestions to help you outreach.

1.   Check the telephone book for local affiliates of national disability groups such as American Council of the Blind, Association of Retarded Citizens, Disabled American Veterans, Epilepsy Foundation of America, Multiple Sclerosis Association, Muscular Dystrophy Association, National Association of the Deaf, National Federation of the Blind, and Paralyzed Veterans of America.

2.   Check the telephone book for local, indigenous groups of people who are disabled or handicapped. These are groups which may not have a national affiliation but are strictly at the grassroots level. Look for listings beginning with "disabled," "disabled citizens," "blind," "vision impaired," "deaf," "hearing impaired," "independent living," "center for independent living," "paralyzed," "muscular," "speech impaired," "neurology," "epilepsy," as well as old standbys "retarded," "retarded citizens," "handicapped," or "handicapped citizens."

The local groups may also be found in the classified pages under "disability," "disability services," or "handicapping services" as well possibly in the front special feature pages of the classifieds under "handicapped," "disability," "disability related services," "health," "rehabilitation, rehabilitation engineering" or even "human services."

3. Check with state and local government agencies. This is multi-pronged. You need to check the state/local unemployment and vocational rehabilitation agencies as well as committees and commissions on handicapped or disabled individuals.

4. Check with employers who are known to have successful equal employment opportunity programs, especially programs that have attracted persons with disabilities. Learn from their success. The groups of people with disabilities may be able to point you to the "better" employers.

5. Social service agencies should also be checked. They have persons with disabilities as clients. Do not assume all are strictly sectarian. For example, many Jewish social agencies provide services to non-Jews as well as to Jews. These are agencies which are providing services to people who want jobs. If they do not have particular people immediately available, they can point you to projects where you may find them.

6. Training projects in the schools or in the private sector are also a good source. Employment opportunity and information centers (OICs) can help with the outreach. Projects with industries (PWI), such as in the electronics industry, are also good sources. Industry associations can lead you to the projects.

7. There are know several areas served by local disability focussed newspapers which will run classified job announcements. Ask disabled persons and concerned organizations for the paper nearest you.

8. When you find an entity to which you are outreaching, ask it for the names of other concerned organizations.

9. Last, but not least, use common sense. Think about the job and where a person with disabilities might learn about it in your community. You know your area. Tap it for you.

Questions That Can Be Asked

It is important that both employers and employees realize that it is necessary to go through an interviewing process. The process should reveal the needed information in terms of the person's ability to do a job. Previously, it has been noted that pre-employment medical inquiries were generally prohibited. That is crucial. Employers should take care to avoid asking questions unrelated to the essential duties of the job. Employers should generally avoid inquiries related to health and disabilities unless absolutely job related, consistent with business necessity.

It must be noted that an employer has the right and duty to inquire about a person's ability to do a job. Given that, the employer should ask certain questions.

Prospective and current employees should answer all questions truthfully. Deliberate untruthfulness may be the basis of an employer refusing to hire or taking disciplinary action against a current employee.

Here are some commonly asked key questions.

1. What is your attendance record at school or at your present job?
2. Do you have a license to _____? (Fill in the blank with a license necessary for the job, e.g., driver or chauffeur's license.)
3. Where did you go to school and why?
4. What organizations are you affiliated with now, or have you been affiliated with in the past, as a volunteer which show your experience or qualifications for the position for which you have applied?
5. Who referred you here?
6. What are your personal and professional goals?
7. State the names, addresses, and telephone numbers of your previous employers and why you took and why you left each job.

8. Do you have the ability to perform on time the essential tasks and duties of the position for you which you applied or wish consideration?
9. On what basis do you believe you are qualified for the position(s) for which you applied or wish consideration?
10. What work experience(s) have you had that make you qualified for the position(s) for which you have applied or wish consideration?
11. What are your employment strengths and weaknesses as related to this job?
12. Are you willing to accept employment, on condition that you pass a job related physical examination?

These questions are not a "dozen dirty tricks" employers may use to obtain information about a person's disability. Rather, each goes to a legitimate purpose regarding the performance of duties and the employer's personnel practices.

Employers should take care to avoid asking unnecessary and unrelated questions. Employers should generally avoid inquires related to health and disabilities unless absolutely job related, consistent with business necessity (preferably documented before the hiring announcement or interview).

A Few No-Nos

While there are definitely questions that can and should be asked, there are also questions which most definitely should NOT be asked. Here are some questions not to be asked UNLESS THE QUESTION RELATES TO A BONA FIDE OCCUPATIONAL QUALIFICATION CONSISTENT WITH BUSINESS NECESSITY. In that most rare circumstance, in which an employer may believe it needs to ask one of these taboo questions, employers are best advised BEFORE making the inquiry to consult legal counsel and to have detailed documentation justifying the question.

1. Do you have a physical or mental handicap or disability?
2. How did you become disabled?

3. Would you need special or expensive accommodations to do the job for which you have applied?
4. Do you have epilepsy, multiple sclerosis, etc.?
5. What medication, if any, do you take on a regular basis?
6. Are there any restrictions on your driver's license?
7. Do you commonly get tired at work in the afternoon?
8. Are you often too tired to get to work on time in the morning?
9. Can you travel independently?
10. Do any of your children, your spouse, or others in your family have physical or mental handicaps?
11. Have you ever had a seizure, heart attack, etc.?
12. Is your diet restricted for any reason?

A Final Note

The employment process is so very much a process of people, disabled and non-disabled, interacting with people, disabled and non-disabled. It is complicated and the glass can be half full or half empty, depending on your perspective.

EMPLOYERS MUST ASK JOB RELATED QUESTIONS THAT ARE CONSISTENT WITH BUSINESS NECESSITY.

EMPLOYEES AND APPLICANTS MUST ANSWER TRUTHFULLY.

ACCESSIBILITY: PUBLIC ACCOMMODATIONS AND ARCHITECTURAL BARRIERS

Introduction

A few years ago, the Washington Post was reporting a lawsuit concerning the local federal courthouse in Alexandria, Virginia. "Handicapped Win Access To Courts," the Post headlined over a picture which told the larger story. While the headline led readers to expect a picture of a person in a wheelchair or on crutches, the picture was of an apparently non-disabled woman pushing a stroller containing an apparently non-disabled baby along the ramp that had been installed as a result of the litigation.

There was no one "handicapped" in the photograph. Yet the "handicapped" design clearly was benefitting non-disabled users: the baby and her parent. Traditionally, accessibility has been perceived as for "the handicapped." Pragmatically, as the Washington Post picture illustrates, accessibility is for everyone—persons with disabilities, elderly persons, the very young, as well as the non-disabled.

Architectural barriers are, in a workable definition, those physical barriers which impede a person from getting from here to there independently, in a functional, safe, and convenient manner. Access means the ability to approach, enter, and use a structure.

An inaccessible environment is, quite literally, threshold discrimination. Access for a person with disabilities gives that individual the power to be an equal participant interacting with peers. Without access to the office and to the worksite there can no equal employment opportunity. Without access in the public school, disabled children, teachers, and administrators are excluded.

This chapter will address accessibility—architectural barrier laws and technical standards, the bricks and mortar of it all. This includes mandates related to places open to the public, places of "public accommodation." This chapter also contains practical guides on how to check for the application of the law as well as the accessibility of a particular structure and site.

It is important at the outset to see accessibility as part of the process. When it is included in the design or conceptual phase of a project it is easier and less costly to implement. In brief, it is far more cost effective to change a line on a blueprint than to rip out a wall. Planning for accessibility is essential.

Ironically, it was a lack of planning that may well have led to the dawning of the age of accessibility.

In 1957 Hugh Deffner, an Oklahoman in a wheelchair, was to receive the award of the President's Committee on Employment of the Handicapped as the Handicapped American of the Year from President Eisenhower. The award was presented in the old United States Department of Labor Building which had only stepped entrances. Mr. Deffner had to be carried up the steps by two Marines to enter the building to participate.

The incident had the effect of catalyzing a series of events which culminated in the development and publication by 1961 of the initial technical standard for accessibility in buildings and facilities. That standard, now known as the American National Standard Institute ("ANSI") A117.1, Specifications for Making Buildings Accessible to, and Usable [sic.] by, the Physically Handicapped, has remained a leading accessibility tool even as it has been reviewed and expanded, with the latest edition being issued in 1986. It will be reviewed and reissued in 1991. The development of the standard foreshadowed the adoption of the federal and state laws, the next focus here. These laws are analyzed in terms of which buildings are to be made accessible under which circumstances and how access is to be achieved.

Federal Mandates For Accessibility

There are three key federal statutes: the Americans with Disabilities Act ("ADA"), the Architectural Barriers Act ("ABA") and the Rehabilitation Act ("Rehab Act").

The ADA, with which we begin, is sweeping 1990 legislation, applying broadly to the design, construction, and alteration of old and new, owned and leased structures. Unlike the ABA or Rehab Act, ADA applies to everyday activities in the private sector, even in the absence of a federal grant or contract.

The ADA in Title III prohibits discrimination against qualified individuals with disabilities in the full and equal enjoyment of the goods, services, facilities, privileges, advantages and accommodations by owners/operators/lessors/lessees of buildings and facilities that are open to the public. Legalistically these are known as places of "public accommodation."

Under ADA individuals with a disability means persons with a physical or mental disability that substantially limits a major life activity, who have a record of such an impairment, or persons regarded as having such an impairment. This is an accepted definition historically rooted in the Rehab Act.

"Public accommodation" is very broadly defined in ADA. Places of public accommodation are places that are open to the public for lodging, food and drink, entertainment, meetings, or to sell to the public. Thus the term encompasses hotels, motels, inns, restaurants, bars, motion picture houses, theatres, auditoria, convention centers, grocery stores, shopping center and other retail sales establishments. Places of public accommodation are also places where services are provided—banks, lawyers' offices, doctors' offices and other health care providers' offices, hospitals. Places of recreation or exercise – parks, zoo, gyms, spas – are also included in the law. Places of public display, such as galleries, museums, and libraries, and social service centers – daycare or senior citizen centers, homeless shelters – are also within the ADA definition of public accommodation. Private schools and transportation terminals are also covered by Title III of ADA. (The provisions in ADA Titles II and III related to transportation vehicles and services are discussed in Chapter 6). There are no exemptions based on size.

The definition does not include religious institutions or entities controlled by religious institutions as well as private clubs.

ADA Title III seeks to ensure that persons with disabilities have equality of opportunity to access, use, and enjoy the goods, services, privileges, and be participants in public accommodations in the most integrated setting appropriate to the needs of the individual.

Title III of ADA is effective January 26, 1992, with regulations to be issued by the Attorney General by July 26, 1991, one year after ADA was enacted. The United States Architectural Transportation Barriers Compliance Board ("ATBCB") was required to issue Minimum Guidelines and Requirements for Accessible Design (MGRAD), upon which the Attorney General's regulation is to be based, by April 26, 1991, nine months after ADA was adopted.

Places of public accommodation and commercial facilities that are designed and constructed for first occupancy after January 26, 1993, (30 months after enactment of the ADA) must be readily accessible to and usable by persons with disabilities except if that is structurally impracticable. (This is a very limited exception embracing situations in which the physical integrity of the structure would be affected, such as could occur with a building on a very steep grade.) Even if the entire facility cannot be made readily accessible and usable to people with disabilities, then those portions which can be made accessible should be.

Under Title III of the ADA, when a place of public accommodation or a commercial facility is altered, the altered area must be readily accessible and usable to the maximum extent feasible. Under ADA there are instances when more than the altered area must be accessible and usable to persons with disabilities. Where the alteration affects a primary function of the facility, ADA requires, to the maximum extent feasible, that the alteration be accessible and usable. In such case, the path of travel to the altered area AND the bathrooms, telephones, and drinking fountains serving the remodeled area also must be readily accessible and usable if to do so would not be disproportionate to the overall alterations in cost and scope. Primary functions of a structure would include the public areas, such as viewing areas of a gallery, customer service area or lobby of a bank, dining area of a cafeteria, meeting rooms of a conference center. By contrast, the boiler room, storage area, mechanical rooms are not primary function areas. The Attorney General is establishing criteria for such decisions, though the legislative history of ADA indicates a cost factor of 30 percent as the benchmark. In essence, ADA distinguishes between minor and major renovations and renovations affecting public usage functions and those involving internal building servicing type functions.

Under the ADA requirements for access in public accommodations and commercial facilities, it is critical to note that elevators are NOT required in facilities that are less than three (3) stories or that have less than 3,000 square feet per story unless the building is a shopping mall, the professional office of a health care provider, or unless the Attorney General of the United States determines that a particular category of such facilities requires the installation of elevators based on the usage of such facilities.

It is a violation of ADA not to remove structural architectural and communication barriers in existing public accommodations where such removal is readily achievable, that is when it can be accomplished without difficulty or expense. If removal of a barrier is not readily achievable, then an entity covered by ADA Title III must use alternative methods that are so achievable to make the goods, services, facilities, privileges, advantages or accommodations available. Whether a particular barrier removal is readily achievable will entail examining the nature and cost of the actions, the overall financial resources of the facilities or facilities involved, the number of persons employed at such facility and the effect on expenses and resources, or other impact of the action on the operation of the facility. The overall size of the entity, in terms of financial resources, facilities, and employees, also is to be considered. A final factor is the type of operation(s) of the entity undertaking the removal and the geographic separateness, administrative or fiscal relationship of the facilities.

In essence, these are the same factors as are to be considered in determining whether an undue hardship precludes making a reasonable accommodation in employment (Chapter 2).

There are additional parallels and similarities to the employment related provisions in other titles of ADA. Title IV of ADA, mandating telecommunication relay services for speech and hearing impaired persons by July 26, 1993, will help employers and owners/operators of places of public accommodation required to remove barriers by making this type of auxiliary service more readily available. Like entities covered by the employment, mandates under Title I, entities covered by ADA Title III cannot do indirectly—by contract or other administrative arrangement—what they are not permitted to do directly. As under Title I, individuals with disabilities need not engage in futile gestures, such as to seek admission to a place of public accommodation, if the individual has actual notice that a person/organization does not intend to comply. Also as under Title I, an individual may not be discriminated against because of the known disability of a person with whom the individual is known to associate or have a relationship. As state and local government make their services, activities and programs (including employment and construction) available on a nondiscriminatory basis (complying with the Attorney General's Title II regulation to be issued by July 26,

1991), more of their new and older buildings and facilities containing program services will be made accessible.

Providers and builders should be alert to evolving technology in removing barriers. Audio descriptions, new and increasing in use in museums, galleries and public television, help provide vision impaired persons access to exhibits and movies. Audio descriptions (oral narrations) help vision impaired persons in the same vein that closed captioning (special printed text) aids hearing impaired persons. Both methods utilize special equipment which helps only those who need assistance and does not affect the general public.

Providers and builders should be aware that Uniform Federal Accessibility Standard ("UFAS") has been accepted as the standard under the other federal laws that are critical in this area, the Rehabilitation Act and Architectural Barriers Act. UFAS will be the point of departure for accessibility standards and MGRAD under ADA. In fact, ADA provides that if regulations have not been issued to implement the public accommodations provisions, and a building permit issues, UFAS should be followed in undertaking alterations or new construction within one year after the issuance of the permit. The exception to this is if the ATBCB has issued its MGRAD for purposes of ADA, and no final rules issue for Title III for a year after that, then compliance should be with the MGRAD.

Readers should also be alert that a state or local government may have their building code or law certified by the Attorney General, in consultation with the ATBCB, as meeting the accessibility requirements under ADA. There must be a public hearing at which persons with disabilities have the opportunity to testify prior to such certification. In any subsequent proceeding alleging a violation of ADA, compliance with such a certified state or local code would be a defense that could be asserted, though it would be subject to rebuttal.

The ADA is a traditional civil rights bill. Thus, the prohibition against discrimination in places of public accommodation entails more than the structural requirements previously noted. ADA seeks to ensure qualified persons with disabilities have the opportunity to participate in and to utilize public accommodations in the most integrated setting appropriate. Under ADA Title III it is also discriminatory to impose/apply eligibility criteria that screen out or tend to screen out an individual with a disability unless the criteria can be shown to be necessary for the provision of the goods or services being offered. It is discriminatory not to make reasonable modifications in the rules, policies and procedures in order to afford individuals with disabilities meaningful opportunity unless the requisite modifications would fundamentally alter the nature of the program. Likewise auxiliary aids and services must be provided unless that too would fundamentally alter the program or would be an undue burden. (These mandates are quite similar to the "program accessibility" requirements of the Rehabilitation Act, discussed later in this chapter.) Qualified persons with disabilities must be afforded equality of benefits and opportunities, which, in general, must not be different or separate from those provided others who are not disabled.

Under ADA it is expressly not discrimination to deny accommodations to an individual who poses a significant risk to the health or others which risk cannot be eliminated by providing auxiliary aids or services or by modifying policies, practices or procedures.

It must be noted that ADA Title III gives an individual the right to go to court for an injunction to obtain specific relief to redress discrimination in a place of public accommodation. Attorney's fees are recoverable. The individual may not recover damages. The Attorney General of the United States may recover compensatory (not punitive) damages, along with injunctive and specific relief, and even a civil penalty (which may be mitigated by the covered entity's good faith efforts to comply with ADA) where there is a pattern and practice of violating Title III of ADA. Except for enforcement actions relating to new construction and alterations that are undertaken by covered entities, enforcement of the public accommodation provision phases in over the first year after Title III becomes effective. During the first six months after the effective date (i.e., until July 26, 1992) enforcement actions may not be brought against businesses that employ 25 or fewer employees and have gross receipts of $1,000,000 or less. If the business has 10 or fewer employees and gross receipts of $500,000 or less, no action may be brought against it until January 26, 1993, one year after the effective date of the provisions.

Title II of ADA forbids discrimination and requires accessibility in the programs, activities and services of state and local government entities. This includes the design, construction and alteration of facilities in which state/local programs, services or activities are offered. The Attorney General is to issue regulations to implement Title II by July 26, 1991. The provisions will go into effect January 26, 1992. It is expected UFAS will be the technical starting point under Title II.

The Americans with Disabilities Act combines principles related to the design and construction of buildings and facilities with traditional civil rights. Viewed in that context, it is the natural evolution of the two other major federal laws, the Architectural Barriers Act and the Rehabilitation Act.

The Architectural Barriers Act was adopted in 1968 and requires federal and federally funded buildings and facilities to be readily accessible to, and usable by, handicapped persons in accordance with standards that are to be prescribed. The ABA covers buildings designed, constructed or altered by, or on behalf of the United States, buildings leased by the United States after January 1, 1977, including renewals of old leases, buildings financed with a federal grant or loan if the building is subject to design and construction standards, as well as the buildings and facilities of the Washington, D.C., Metro Transit System are all covered by the ABA. As originally enacted, the law did not apply to leased buildings unless they were leased after design/construction in accordance with federal plans and specifications. The law was changed in 1976 to expand the coverage of the Act to embrace more leased buildings.

Buildings which are open to the public or where handicapped persons may be employed must be accessible. The term "building" in the ABA was intended to have a broad meaning and embraces recreational, medical, educational, and other structures, above and beyond office facilities of the federal government. Excluded from the ABA mandate of accessibility are structures intended primarily for non-disabled military personnel as well as privately owned residential structures (other than those structures leased by the government for subsidized housing).

Under the ABA, as originally enacted, three agencies, the Department of Housing and Urban Development with respect to residential structures, the Department of Defense with respect to military facilities, and the General Services Administration with respect to all other facilities and buildings, issue access standards. The agencies issued standards approximately a year after the law was adopted. A 1976 amendment to the ABA authorizes the United States Postal Service to issue standards for its buildings and facilities. The head of each agency issuing a standard is authorized to waive or modify that access standard on a case by case basis when it is clearly necessary.

In issuing accessibility standards the federal agencies all predicated their work on the original 1961 ANSI standard.

Until 1984 the standards did vary among the four agencies. With respect to pre-1985 projects it is important to be alert to the particular standard in effect at the time the contract/grant was awarded so as to be sure what exactly was required.

In 1984 the four agencies issuing standards under the ABA issued the "federal" standard, the Uniform Federal Accessibility Standard ("UFAS"), which was based on Minimum Guidelines and Requirements for Accessible Design that had been developed by the United States Architectural Barriers Compliance Board ("ATBCB"). ATBCB was established by section 502 of the Rehabilitation Act to ensure compliance with the standards issued under the ABA. UFAS is intended to bring consistency and uniformity to federal and federally funded design and construction. A common approach in all types of structures is being taken by the four previously somewhat divergent standards.

The ABA is enforceable in several ways. The agency issuing the funding grant/contract can and should always take appropriate actions to ensure that the access requirement, like other mandates, is met. The ATBCB is a separate, administrative agency within the federal government that can initiate legal proceedings resulting in funds being cut off or corrective action being required. The ATBCB proceedings are informal, due process hearings before an Administrative Law Judge, with an appeal to the court.

However, it is also possible to go to court directly. Cases have been successful in enjoining the use of facilities that were accessible to non-disabled persons but not in compliance with access mandates for persons with disabilities. The inclusion of operational accessibility features has been judicially compelled. Structures open to the public and where persons with disabilities may be employed which are leased by the government, including the United States Postal Service, must be accessible when those structures open, not when and if the structure is subsequently altered. Merely planning for access does not comply with the law. Moreover, successful plaintiffs have been awarded attorney's fees.

The ABA is prospective in operation. It is not a mandate to go back into older buildings and renovate them to make them barrier free. The underlying philosophy is that when work is done on a structure, it must be accessible and usable, in accordance with the standards that have been issued. Under the limited approach of the ABA, new buildings are accessible when they are designed and constructed. Older buildings achieve greater access when they are altered.

The Rehabilitation Act takes a broader approach to accessibility and programs for qualified disabled persons, which includes persons with either a physical or mental impairment which substantially limits a major life activity.

Title V of the Rehabilitation Act contains the landmark civil rights protections for qualified persons with disabilities. Under section 504 qualified persons with disabilities may not be excluded from any program or activity receiving federal financial assistance (grant, loan, etc.) or, as a result of amendments in 1978, from any program or activity of the federal government. An inaccessible building is discriminatory because it prohibits an otherwise willing individual from being a participant.

To implement section 504 each federal agency issues regulations applicable to the recipients of its federal aid as well as to its own programs. Historically these were developed by the Department of Health, Education, and Welfare which initially was the lead federal agency under Title V, a responsibility shifted in 1980 to the Department of Justice.

As a general rule each federal agency required compliance with ANSI A117.1-1961(r.1971) in the design and construction of new buildings and facilities as well as when undertaking alterations with federal aid. The regulations generally permit compliance with other methods where it is clearly evident that equivalent access will be provided. In 1988 the Department of Justice revised the federal 504 regulation to provide that a building meeting UFAS standard complied with the Rehabilitation Act. Other federal agencies also made the change to UFAS in their regulations. One major federal program, that of the Office of Revenue Sharing, accepted adherence to the 1980 edition of the ANSI A117.1 standard.

As a general rule, the federal agencies' rules define "facilities" to include the building, structures, equipment, roads, parking lot, or other real and personal property. New buildings are to be barrier free or fully accessible. Alteration projects must be similarly accessible. In these respects the Rehabilitation Act takes an approach similar to the Architectural Barriers Act, though there are no waivers under the Rehab Act. The enforcement approach, both in terms of sanctions and remedies available is also the same, though the ATBCB has no statutory enforcement role under section 504. Compliance incentives under the federal laws are discussed in conjunction with the state laws later in this chapter.

The most profound difference between the two statutes concerns buildings which predate the mandate of the laws. Under the ABA an older (pre-1969) structure which is not leased now or which is not altered is not required to be accessible. However, under the Rehab Act, programs within such a structure, including employment opportunities, must be accessible. The practical result is that at least parts of older structures have had to be renovated and made accessible. The Rehab Act is similar to ADA, in that under the public accommodations provisions (Title III) and state and local government activities and programs (Title II) older (as well as all new) structures must be accessible and usable.

The regulations which implement section 504 allow flexibility in achieving program accessibility. It is NOT necessary to totally gut and redo a structure. Program accessibility can be achieved, without undertaking total renovations, by consolidating the available services and opportunities on the first floor of a multi-story building or into one of two facilities offering the same services. Either approach would obviate the need to provide full accessibility in the structure where the program was contained on one floor or to make both older structures accessible where the program was fully within one of them. Congress reiterated this when it amended the Rehab Act in 1988 (in conjunction with the adoption of the Civil Rights Restoration Act). It made clear that small providers (less than 15 employees) are not required to make significant structural alterations of existing facilities to achieve program accessibility if alternative means of providing the services are available.

The key to understanding program access under section 504 with respect to older buildings is to focus on the program/activity and the services and opportunities it affords, NOT the older structure. The former, not the latter, must be available to qualified persons with disabilities.

A Few Final Notes In Passing From The Rehab Act

First, observe that in contrast to the ABA, the Rehab Act does not treat leased buildings in any special manner. Leased buildings are not mentioned in the statute or agency regulations. A leased building containing a program/activity that is federally funded must have the program/activity accessible, not necessarily the entire leased structure.

Second, the extension of the Rehab Act to the programs and activities of the federal government means that as a practical matter, as those agencies comply with the Rehab Act, more older federal structures will inevitably be modified for access.

Also bear in mind that under the Rehabilitation Act government contractors are required to take affirmative action in hiring and promoting qualified disabled persons. This is section 503, administered by the Department of Labor and discussed in Chapter 2. At this point it is important that no standard for physical access in the workplace is set forth in the implementing regulations of the Department of Labor, though the Department initially applied ANSI A-117.1 as the technical standard. It is now looking to UFAS.

Two other federal laws worth briefly noting. Public Law 100-641, adopted in late 1988, requires the Department of Transportation develop a uniform system of handicapped parking regulations. The International Symbol of Accessibility (see cover) is the official symbol for identifying vehicles transporting people with disabilities. The parking regulations are to be issued in 1991. ADA requires the Attorney General in coordination with the Secretary of Transportation and the ATBCB to develop a technical assistance plan for implementing the public accommodations provisions (other than those noted in Chapter 6 related to transit vehicles and services) by January 22, 1991. This plan is the appropriate place to coordinate implementation of the DOT parking rules and ADA.

The other significant federal law is the 1984 Voting Accessibility for the Elderly and Handicapped Act which requires all polling places for federal elections (general, primary, special) be accessible to temporarily or permanently physically handicapped voters. Each state must also have a reasonable number of accessible permanent registration facilities.

State laws relating to accessibility also will be applicable under federal grants and contracts as those documents routinely provide for the recipient or contractor to comply with all applicable federal, state, and local laws. State laws come into the picture very early in the process and it is to those laws that we now turn.

State Laws

Every state, as seen in Appendix I, has a law requiring accessibility for persons with disabilities in buildings. Many state accessibility laws apply to private structures, i.e., structures where there is no state financial or physical presence. State laws apply to buildings that are owned or funded by the state and also to many structures which are open to the public.

State laws also generally have a process to obtain waivers of requirements based upon undue hardship or impracticability. States may expressly exempt smaller structures from certain requirements, e.g., not requiring access to both stories of a structure less than 4000 square feet.

States most commonly use the ANSI A117.1 standard in combination with their own requirements. See Appendix I setting forth the standard in each state. The trend in the states definitely has been to the 1980 and 1986 editions of ANSI, though several states use other editions of this ANSI standard. Some states, such as California and New Hampshire adhere to their own code and do not use ANSI. Ohio, Virginia and Vermont are examples of states which use ANSI in concert with other standards. Certain states, e.g., Hawaii, use the latest edition of ANSI with other provisions unique to their jurisdiction. Bear in mind that ANSI

A117.1 will be reviewed and reissued in 1991. Despite the clear trend to ANSI A117.1, there is certainly no uniformity and each state code must be checked.

States also have laws prohibiting discrimination in places of public accommodation. Those laws are also identified in Appendix I. These laws, which are already in effect, are quite similar to the provisions in Title III of the Americans with Disabilities Act discussed earlier in this chapter. While most of these laws are traditional civil/human rights anti-discrimination laws, in several states, such as Arizona and Florida, the applicable law is the White Cane Law. Buildings which complied with state/local building codes when they were constructed are generally considered to be in compliance with the state public accommodations law. Some states may have both anti-discrimination and White Cane laws.

Readers are cautioned that the definition of place of public accommodation, while generally similar to the definition in the Americans with Disabilities Act noted above, does vary in each state law. The remedies and penalties for violating the nondiscrimination laws related to places of public accommodation also vary from state to state. The range of relief may encompass damages as well as specific and injunctive relief. Another variable is whether the nondiscrimination law is enforceable by the state agency in proceedings before the agency or by the individual directly in court. White Cane laws are traditionally criminal in nature, enforceable by the state attorney general. Offenses are a relatively minor crime, a misdemeanor. There are exceptions, such as California, which allows the individual wronged to maintain a civil action for violations.

State accessibility requirements should be available from state and local building authorities as well as the state committee on employment of persons with disabilities, often known as the Governor's Committee on Employment of People with Disabilities. Many of these are also noted in Appendix I as points of contact.

Compliance Incentives

Traditionally incentives to comply with laws come in the negative. If you do not comply, then untoward things happen to you. In the present context, the consequences of noncompliance with accessibility requirements can be serious. Judicial enforcement, discussed under the federal law, is always available with a loss of eligibility or cut off of federal/state funding or compliance order, with award of attorney's fees possible. At the state/local level, most practically, a building permit or certificate of occupancy can be withheld from a noncomplying building. This can impede totally the processes of building and using a structure. At the building permit stage the design is checked. At the certificate of occupancy stage the actual construction is reviewed for compliance. These are fundamental documents which must be obtained.

There are also positive incentives. Under federal law there was a $35,000 tax deduction for removal of architectural, transportation, or communication barriers. In late 1990, tax legislation was enacted giving small businesses (30 or fewer employees and less than $1 million gross sales) operating places of public accommodation a tax credit of up to $5,000 per year for providing auxiliary aids and services to their disabled employees. The architectural barrier removal deduction was reduced to a maximum of $15,000, as of January 1, 1991, when the auxiliary aid tax credit became effective. The barrier removal deduction is not available for new construction. A few states also provide tax incentives.

Perhaps the greatest incentives must be in the context of the overall design of structures. An accessible structure is available to the greatest number of potential users. Major facilities, such as the Smithsonian Museum, have developed brochures detailing their accessibility as part of their serving the public. The Washington Post story of a victory for the "handicapped" featured the baby carriage brigade in the photograph utilizing the ramp. Good signage in a building, while essential for a person who is hearing impaired, in fact helps everyone get around the structure. Grab bars and hand rails at sinks in bathrooms are safety features for everyone, not only those people with balance problems. A reinforced wall may later facilitate converting the unit into one a person with disabilities can use. Auditory cues and raised letters can be aesthetically pleasing as well as appropriate in crowded areas, such as terminals, stadia, or offices. Volume enhancement on a telephone at an airport or a train station is almost a necessity, whatever your hearing. "Handicapped" design can be truly universal design and benefit more than the immediately known audience.

Coping: Points To Remember

1.   Planning is critical. Develop a team including design and legal personnel who are knowledgeable about the subject.

2.   Apply the standard for all types of disabilities—vision, hearing, mobility, coordination, etc.

3.   Keep in mind whether the audience is adults or children. The standards are based on adults and you have to adapt them for children. Access standards that consider the size of children will be developed in the next few years.

4.   New structures have to be fully, not partially, accessible. Building permits and certificates of occupancy can be withheld.

5.   Until January 26, 1992, for federal law to be applicable, there must be a federal presence in either funds, ownership, program, activity, lease.

6.   Beginning January 26, 1992, Title II of ADA applies prohibiting discrimination and mandating accessibility in state and local government programs, services and activities even if there is no federal financial link by a contract or grant.

7.   Also beginning January 26, 1992, Title III of ADA applies to private structures that are public accommodations, mandating access even if there is no federal financial link. Title III places of public accommodations or commercial facilities designed or constructed for furst occupancy after January 26, 1993, must, as

a general rule, be accessible to and usable by persons with disabilities.

8. All states have access codes. Access is going to be required even if the federal law is inapplicable. Should both be applicable, the federal prevails in case of conflict.

9. A structure is likely to have a useful life of at least 40 years. Consider the potential users in its lifetime.

10. Consider accessibility as a regular part of the maintenance and improvement of a facility and check the federal and state tax codes when undertaking such work.

11. Access standards were developed originally with office buildings in mind. The access standards for theaters, cafeterias, libraries and other special use areas have emerged more recently. Designers and builders are thus least experienced with them. These areas are particularly susceptible to pitfalls.

12. Keep in mind that with respect to older buildings, program accessibility puts the emphasis on the program of services, not the structure. In new structures the rule is full access.

13. Think functionally in terms of people approaching, entering and using a structure independently, safely, and conveniently, be the people disabled or non-disabled.

14. Utilize solutions which, while solving the problem for one group of persons with disabilities, do not create a problem for another. For example, when setting visual alarms to warn persons who are hearing impaired of an emergency, make sure that the frequency of the flashing light is not one which will cause persons with epilepsy to start having seizures. Curb ramps should have a different texture from sidewalk so that persons who are vision impaired can detect the change of surface and realize they are in the street.

Applicability Of Access Code Form

Here is a simple form you can utilize to determine the applicability of access codes to a particular project. Complete as many lines as are applicable.

Name of Project:
Location:

I. Project Basics
    a. New Construction
    b. Alteration
    c. Addition
    d. Number of Levels
    e. Square Footage
    f. Lease Term
II. Funding
    a. Federal
    b. State/Local
    c. Private
    d. Mixed
III. Owner
    a. Federal
    b. State/Local
    c. Private
IV. Type of Structure
    a. Office Building
    b. Residential
    c. Government Only
    d. Government/Private Mixed Use
    e. Single Unit
    f. Multiple Units
    g. Postal Facility
    h. Park/Recreational
    i. Hospital/Medical
    j. Other (Specify)

V.   Users/Restrictions
    a. Public at Large
    b. Business Invitee (Workers and Public)
    c. Employees Only
    d. Special Restrictions (Specify)
VI. Special Use Areas
    a. Offices
    b. Cafeteria
    c. Assembly
    d. Medical
    e. Recreational
    f. Library
    g. Other: (Specify)
VII. Additional Concerns/Notes

Approaching Access Standards: Technical Considerations Form

As previously noted, there are a number of accessibility standards. To determine whether a particular building is in compliance it is important to know what standard is applicable and whether that standard is being followed. Not all standards are alike, though ANSI and UFAS are at the fore. Here are some general considerations which can be checked on all structures. This is not a guaranteed checklist, rather a functional point of departure for reviewing a building for accessibility in accordance with the particular standard a jurisdiction has made applicable.

Outside/Approach
1. Grading level at entrance.
2. Parking, if provided, proximate to entrance.
3. Number of accessible parking spaces and total spaces.
4. Gradient of walks.
5. Blending of walks to other surfaces/platforms.
6. Width of walks.
7. Surface slip resistant/nonslip.
8. Accessible route to primary entrance.
9. Accessible route connecting accessible elements/facilities.
10. Accessible route from primary entrance to public transportation.

Ramps
1. Slope.
2. Length.
3. Handrails — length, height, extension, which side(s).
4. Surface — slip resistant/nonslip.
5. Width.
6. Clearances at top/bottom.
7. Cross slope.
8. Edge protection.
9. Rest area dimensions.

Entrances
1. Numbers – total and number accessible.
2. Number of accessible routes to accessible elevators.
3. Number of primary entrances.

Doors
1. Clear opening.
2. Pressure necessary to open.
3. Extension/swing.
4. Level changes/inclines at doorsill.
5. Threshold heights.

Stairs
1. Number of risers and height of each.
2. Handrails – length, height, extensions, which side(s).
3. Protruding lips/abrupt nosings.

Floors
1. Slip resistant or nonslip surface.
2. If covered, by what and how attached.
3. Common level linked by ramps.

Toilets
1. Number of facilities for each sex, total on each floor.
2. Number of facilities for disabled persons of each sex on each floor.
3. Number of unisex bathrooms total.
4. Number of accessible unisex bathrooms.
5. Clear space for persons in wheelchairs.
6. Width of stall.
7. Door swing of stall.
8. Handrails.
9. Grab bars.
10. Height of toilet seat.
11. Reachable flush controls. Height. Operability.
12. Height of urinal.
13. Height of mirror above floor.
14. Height of towel dispenser above floor.

15. Height of disposal units above floor.
16. Sink controls – levered, automatic.
17. Pipes – covered, insulated, temperature controlled.
18. Shower/bath – entrance, exit, controls, seating.

Water Fountains
1. Number accessible per floor.
2. Controls.
3. Operated by hand or foot.

Public Telephones
1. Number of public telephones total.
2. Number of accessible public telephones.
3. Height of coin slots above floor.
4. Height of dial above floor.
5. How approached by person in wheelchair.
6. Number of telephones with amplifiers.
7. Controls – how operated.
8. Location and number of TTYs (teletypewriters).

Elevator
1. Number accessible and number on accessible route.
2. Height of buttons – inside/outside, including emergency.
3. Tactile cues – at jambs, in car.
4. Auditory cues.
5. Cab dimensions.
6. Length of time door open.
7. Door opening width.
8. Flush with floor.

Controls
1. Height above floor.
2. Force necessary to operate.
3. Forward approach or side approach.
4. Space surrounding.

Identification
1. Raised letters.
2. Height.

3. Distance from door if on a wall.
4. Special identification on doors dangerous for those with visual impairments or doors not otherwise used regularly.

Warning Signals (Alarms)

1. Auditory—decibel level.
2. Visual—light frequency.
3. Simultaneous auditory and visual.

Hazards

1. Exits identified.
2. Low hanging objects.
3. Protrusions.
4. Lighting on exits and ramps.
5. Height clearances along accessible route, in accessible spaces, elements.

Special Elements

The sheer diversity of these facilities makes it impractical to enumerate everything that needs to be reviewed. An effective way to check a special element or different facility, such as a library, is to consider it from a functional viewpoint. Persons with disabilities must be able to enjoy all the facilities independently in a functional, safe, and convenient manner. In the context of the library example that means reaching books, including research materials, traversing aisles, going through security checkouts, as well as the need for an accessible entrance and toilets. Seating would also have to be provided. The same approach can be taken with auditoriums and theaters though access codes may specify the number of viewing positions and seats to be made available. As previously noted, these are potential problem areas since the standards for these areas are newest. Check these items closely with the applicable code sections. They will help make public accommodations accessible to and usable by persons with disabilities.

A Final Note

Accessible design is here to stay in the design codes and the law. While once it was thought of as "handicapped design," there is growing recognition that an accessible environment benefits all, disabled and non-disabled. Eventually accessibility will be so ingrained in the building and design processes that we will accept it as "design" without a second thought, much in the manner that "fuel efficient" cars are accepted as "cars" today.

By breaking down the physical barriers, the attitudinal myths can be dispelled and substantive problems addressed. Accessibility unlocks the door of human potential for persons with disabilities.

Chapter 4

HOUSING

Introduction

A few years ago I was looking for a home in the suburbs of Washington. As I was actively involved in disability issues, I tried to find an accessible house. This proved to be difficult at best, demoralizing at worst.

Earlier, in the Introduction, I related how I found a fully accessible bathroom — at the very top level of a multi-story home. Reachable only by stairs, this upper level was apparently where the person with disabilities was sheltered. This led me to change my house hunting strategy.

I thought it might be easier to work out access in a new home. At one development I asked the sales agent about changes in the floor plan as, for example, a ramp or grade level entrance and a larger, fully accessible bathroom on the first floor. The response was that all changes in the basic design had to be approved by the members of the community who were already living or who had purchased there. The sales person suggested maybe some of the people wouldn't want persons with disabilities living there. I suggested the agent had just exceeded my tolerance level for bigotry and that I didn't choose to live among such people.

A friend in a wheelchair moved to the area and sought an accessible place to live. He would read the newspaper advertisements and was invariably keenly disappointed when he responded to the advertisements that said the housing was accessible. To the people placing the ads, "accessible" meant close to the highway or to the subway system or to good schools and shopping.

Housing for persons with disabilities is not easy to find. The stock of existing housing was built predominantly before provisions relating to housing or dwelling units permeated the accessibility standards and were part of accepted design practices and codes.

Initially the thrust of this chapter is to give an overview of the federal and state laws affecting housing for persons with disabilities. In brief, the network of rights and obligations affecting housing facilities and individuals with disabilities, while already extensive at the state level, has expanded at the federal level in the past few years.

In the latter part of the chapter the nuts and bolts, or, more appropriately, the bricks and mortar, affecting housing are discussed in terms of the elements of an accessible unit as well as "adaptable housing." The latter is a term used for housing for persons with disabilities and embraces the concept of structuring a unit so that it can be easily made accessible at any time by a subsequent user who would so choose. It is the wave of the future and highly significant.

While it is clear there will be more accessible housing in the future, it is also clear that there are now more and more persons in society with disabilities who can afford and require residences, whether such residences are apartments that are leased or owned, or detached structures. Those persons are consumers now and will be for years to come. Thus the laws and standards discussed here are of increasing practical importance.

Federal Law

Federal law affecting housing for persons with disabilities is now in a period of implementation, following a flurry of legislative and regulatory activities. The recent trend was in marked contrast to the extended period of dormancy which preceded it.

Federal rights and responsibilities affecting housing and residential units for persons with disabilities are embodied in four key statutes: Fair Housing Act Amendments of 1988, Rehabilitation Act, Architectural Barriers Act, and, to a limited extent, the Americans with Disabilities Act. There are also substantive program statutes under which federal financial assistance can be made available. However, as a general rule those program statutes are not addressed here.

The Fair Housing Act was amended in 1988 to prohibit discrimination in virtually all routine housing transactions, including, but not limited to, the sale, leasing, enjoyment, financing, brokering, appraising, advertising of residential units. The Act was adopted September 13, 1988, and became effective on March 12, 1989, extending to qualified handicapped individuals (including persons with physical or mental disabilities) the substantive protections which had previously been in effect to prohibit discrimination in housing based on color, religion, sex, or national origin. (The 1988 amendments also banned discrimination on the basis of familial status.) This law seeks to ensure nondiscriminatory opportunity in the terms, conditions, and privileges of housing. The 1988 enactment brought the federal law into substantive harmony with the many state laws noted in Appendix I which also prohibit discrimination in housing against persons with disabilities.

The threshold question in any law is who is covered. It is critical that the definition of "handicap" in the 1988 law includes persons with a physical or mental impairment which substantially limits one or more of such person's major life activities, has a record of such impairment, or a person who is regarded as having such an impairment. The definition excludes current illegal drug users or persons addicted to a controlled substance but does include alcoholics, persons with AIDS and HIV infected individuals as long as the person is otherwise qualified. (This means health and safety considerations, such as discussed in Chapter 2, Employment, are also relevant here.) Until enactment of the 1988 amendments, violations of the Fair Housing Act had been redressable only in the federal courts, where the remedy could include compensatory and punitive damages, injunctive relief, attorney's fees and courts costs. Also, the Attorney General of the United States can bring to court the major cases, including those instances in which there appears to be a pattern or practice of denying rights under this law. There have been federal cases involving wrongful limitations on group homes for disabled persons as well as failure to make reasonable accommodations. The Fair Housing Act Amendments of 1988 added a new forum for redressing potential violations: hearings before Administrative Law Judges of the Department of Housing and Urban Development ("HUD").

The Fair Housing Amendments of 1988 were implemented by HUD in final regulations issued January 23, 1989. HUD's rules make clear that it is unlawful for any person to refuse to permit, at the expense of a handicapped person, reasonable modifications to existing premises that would afford the disabled person full enjoyment of the premises or dwelling. A landlord may, where it is reasonable to do so, condition permission for a modification on the renter agreeing to restore the interior of the premises to the condition that existed before the modification (reasonable wear and tear excepted). The landlord can require a reasonable description of the work to be done, assurances the work will be done in a workmanlike fashion and that all required permits will be obtained. Where appropriate, additional escrow payments, bearing interest for the tenant may be required. The landlord cannot require that work be done by a particular contractor. Nor can the landlord require restoration of an alteration which does not affect the use and enjoyment of the premises by future tenants, such as when a doorway is widened for wheelchair access.

HUD's rules also make clear that the reasonable accommodations in an owner's operations and policies that are necessary to afford a disabled person equal opportunity to use and enjoy a dwelling unit and common areas, are required. For examples, this would include allowing seeing eye dogs in a "no pet" building or a reserved parking space for a mobility impaired individual in a lot that was otherwise "first come, first served." The housing provider or landlord is not required to provide supportive services, counseling, medical, or social services that fall outside the scope of services the provider offers other residents. The correct inquiry for the housing provider and prospective resident is whether, with appropriate modifications, the applicant can live in the housing the provider offers, not whether the applicant could benefit from some other type of housing the provider does not offer.

Multifamily buildings, (generally those buildings with 4 or more units if an elevator is in the building, or, if no elevator then the ground floor units of a building with 4 or more units) for first occupancy after March 13, 1991 (30 months after the Act) must have an accessible route. This means the structure must have a continuous unobstructed path connecting accessible spaces in a building or within a site that can be negotiated by a person with a severe disability or a person in a wheelchair that is also safe for persons with other disabilities, unless it is impractical to do so because of the terrain or unusual characteristics of the site. The March 13, 1991, date applies if the building is occupied by that date or the last building permit (or renewal) is issued by the state/county/local authority by January 13, 1990. Such buildings also must have accessible public, common use areas, doors wide enough to allow passage into and within the premises by persons in wheelchairs, as well as adaptability (capable of being accessible) features such as an accessible route through the covered dwelling unit. This also includes power switches, electrical outlets, and other controls in accessible locations, reinforced walls in bathrooms that would allow installation of grab bars around the facilities provided, bathrooms and kitchens having enough space for persons in wheelchairs to maneuver and use. In its January, 1989, regulations HUD makes clear that the technical aspects of accessibility can be achieved by complying with ANSI A117.1-1986. HUD also provided that compliance with a state or local standard that has these same accessibility requirements would also be compliance with the Fair Housing rules. State accessibility standards are noted in Appendix I. In early 1991, HUD is to issue definitive federal technical access standards for complying with the Fair Housing Act Amendments of 1988 and will likely keep the provisions related to state access codes in effect.

The next most vital federal law affecting housing and persons with disabilities is section 504 of the Rehabilitation Act mandating nondiscrimination in programs of federal financial assistance. Applying section 504 in the context of housing is not too difficult.

Section 504 applies to persons who have a physical or mental impairment which substantially limits one or more major life activities, who have a record of such an impairment, or are regarded as having such an impairment. See Chapter 2, for a more detailed discussion of who is covered by the statutory definition.

Keep in mind that as a result of the Civil Rights Restoration Act of 1988 (CRRA) the emphasis with section 504 is no longer the specific program or activity receiving Federal funds. The mandate for program accessibility now extends to all of a recipient's programs and activities if the recipient of the federal aid is a department, agency, housing authority or other instrumentality of state or local government. If the recipient of the federal aid is a corporation which provides housing services, then section 504's mandate not to discriminate applies to the entire corporation.

CRRA did not affect the well established tenet that there must be accessible housing available in a program which offers housing even if the main purpose of the federal grant is not for housing. While this issue has never arisen, the United States Supreme Court has held that it is illegal to discriminate in employment related to persons with disabilities even when the main purpose of the federal aid was not for employment, *Conrail v. Darrone*, 465 U.S. 24 (1984). The same holding would have resulted if the issue had been housing discrimination. It means that under a grant for housing services, there may not be employment discrimination.

There are several programs in which financial assistance is provided from the federal government for housing. These include college dormitories constructed under grants from the Department of Education, as well as programs administered by the Department of Housing and Urban Development, including the Community Development Block Grant and section 8 voucher programs. Under the latter, a person with a disability is considered a family for purposes of the program and is thus eligible.

It is critical that the requirements for program accessibility in residential structures apply whether or not the funding from the federal government is from the United States Department of Housing and Urban Development or another agency. Recipients are to comply with the requirement of the agency providing the financial assistance. The final HUD regulations implementing section 504 were issued in June 1988, and covered persons with physical or mental impairments as well as persons regarded as having impairments. Persons with disabilities would be considered qualified if they met the basic eligibility and substantive requirements for the program, e.g. age, income and were capable of complying with all obligations of occupancy, either with or without supportive services provided by other than the recipient of federal funds. Under section 504, as under the Fair Housing Act Amendments, recipients of federal funds are not required to provide supportive services, such as counseling, medical, or social services, that are outside the scope of the housing program. The HUD regulation, like the other federal rules implementing section 504, does not require a recipient to make fundamental alterations to its program.

"Program accessibility," the fundamental regulatory concept in the implementation of section 504, in terms of housing, means that the full range of housing units and services must be available to qualified persons with disabilities. It does not mean that all units of the structure, even in new buildings, have to be barrier free. In general, program accessibility means that qualified disabled persons are to have the housing alternatives and choices of living arrangements comparable to others eligible for the federally funded program.

The rule of thumb under the HUD regulation is that new multifamily (5 or more units) projects must be accessible, i.e., in compliance with the Uniform Federal Accessibility Standard, with at least 5 percent (at least one unit) accessible to persons with mobility impairments. (Observe that the definition of multi-family project is different under section 504 for federally assisted housing than for nonfederally funded under the Fair Housing Act.)

Program accessibility also means that some older units may have to be modified to be accessible. Massive, total retrofitting is generally not required. Occupants under existing leases do not have to be displaced. The rule of thumb is 5 percent (minimum 1) of each type of unit, even the older ones, must be in compliance.

A housing unit that is on an accessible route, i.e., a continuous unobstructed path connecting accessible spaces and elements, and adaptable, i.e., capable of being accessible to persons with disabilities, is also considered to be in compliance with the HUD 504 regulation. In addition to the 5 percent (at least one) requirement for mobility impaired persons, 2 percent (at least one) of the units must be accessible for persons with hearing or vision impairments.

It is clear that all elements of the housing program, including advertisement, financing, use of the unit, and related facilities must be available on a nondiscriminatory basis to qualified persons with disabilities. It is also clear that when a unit or residential structure is altered with federal funds, such alteration must be undertaken in a way which will result in accessibility.

New construction and alterations must be done in accordance with the Uniform Federal Accessibility Standard (UFAS) the technical standard in the HUD final section 504 regulation. Note that under UFAS, areas to and around as well as within the units must be accessible. The Department of Justice has made clear that compliance with UFAS by the recipients of federal agencies would be compliance with section 504. Many federal agencies changed their regulations to reflect this.

HUD rules make clear that where substantial alterations are undertaken to a project (including a public housing project) that has 15 or more units and the cost of the alterations is 75 percent or more of the replacement cost of the completed facility, then those substantial alterations are treated as new construction. However, in other multifamily projects alterations are to be readily accessible to and usable by persons with disabilities to the extent feasible. Also, if the alterations of single elements or spaces of a dwelling unit, when considered together, amount to an alteration of the unit, the entire unit has to be accessible. Alterations to common areas or parts of facilities that affect accessibility of existing housing facilities must, to the maximum extent feasible, be accessible and usable by persons with disabilities. Recipients of federal funds had until July, 1991, to make the structural changes necessary to achieve the program accessibility mandate of the HUD 504 regulations.

The Department of Housing and Urban Development also has adopted the UFAS as the standard for residential structures under the Architectural Barriers Act. Under the Architectural Barriers Act, certain federally assisted residential structures must, as required by HUD, meet UFAS and be accessible whether the assistance is from the Department of Housing and Urban Development, or another agency. This requirement embraces programs such as section 8 housing. Also subject to the Architectural Barriers Act are residential structures leased by the federal government in subsidized housing programs. Because of the definition of "building" within the Architectural Barriers Act, the scope of the application of the ABA to residential structures is extremely limited.

Prior to the adoption of UFAS, effective in October, 1984, the standard for residential structures subject to the Architectural Barriers Act had been the ANSI A117.1-1961(r.1971) with some minor variations set forth in the HUD regulations to address features particular to housing.

Under the Architectural Barriers Act as well as section 504 of the Rehabilitation Act the remedies and sanctions for noncompliance are significant. The federal agencies providing the funds can require corrective action, as well as withhold or suspend funding. In addition, affected persons can file complaints with the funding agency to initiate a review of the project for its compliance with accessibility. The courts are also available and may enjoin the occupancy/use or wrong application of the access code in noncomplying projects, as well as award damages and attorney's fees, for violations of section 504. The Architectural Barriers Act requirements are also enforceable in the courts with the full panoply of remedies available.

In certain critical areas the federal government's role is limited. In the area of insured financing or guaranteed loans, as in FHA or VA housing, while the Veterans Administration or HUD may have technical expertise in accessible residential structures and may provide financing, it has no nondiscrimination mandate. Neither program is subject to either section 504 of the Rehabilitation Act or the Architectural Barriers Act.

Finally at the federal level is the Americans with Disabilities Act, which extended the federal nondiscrimination mandate to housing programs and services of state and local governments (Title II) and to places of public accommodation, such as inns, hotels, and motels (Title III). The Title II mandate is effective January 26, 1992, eighteen (18) months after the law was enacted. The Attorney General's regulations on state and local government programs and services were required to be issued by July 26, 1991. The Title III public accommodation regulations were also due by that date. Title III is effective January 26, 1992. New covered housing that is a public accommodation designed or constructed for first occupancy after January 26, 1993, must be accessible and usable. (Public accommodations are discussed at greater length in Chapter 3.)

Recent developments, particularly adoption of the Fair Housing Amendments, issuance of the HUD 504 rules, and the Americans with Disabilities Act, will, when the federal mandates are effective, make the federal law closely parallel the state laws. State laws, considered next, historically to a much greater degree than the federal law, affected the daily interactions of persons providing as well as those needing housing. Notwithstanding the activity at the federal level the past several years, state housing laws remain critical.

State Laws

State laws which prohibit discrimination against persons with disabilities are generally embodied in their generic civil or human rights laws. However, not all states have laws which prohibit discrimination in housing against persons with disabilities. Several statutes are limited in their coverage to persons with physical disabilities and do not apply to persons with mental impairments. See Appendix I for citations to all laws.

The threshold issue in any state law is to whom there is an obligation, or viewed differently, who is protected. Where provision is made in the nondiscrimination law it is most commonly a prohibition from discrimination against persons who are physically or mentally impaired. States such as Delaware, New York, Michigan, and New Mexico have laws along this line. Other states, such as Kentucky, have laws which encompass only those people who are physically handicapped. Colorado, Rhode Island, and Wisconsin have expanded their laws to cover persons who are mentally impaired as well as persons who are physically impaired. Jurisdictions such as Hawaii, Missouri, and Florida statutorily cover person with AIDS. Other states, such as Pennsylvania and Illinois, have interpreted their existing laws to cover persons with AIDS.

The state laws apply to the full gamut of housing related transactions: sale, purchase, rental, financing, and transactions related thereto. State laws prohibit inquiries concerning a person's disability in connection with acquiring, financing, construction, repairing, maintaining, leasing, or rehabilitating a housing unit. Advertising which discriminates is prohibited.

The general thrust of the state civil or human rights laws affecting housing for persons with disabilities is to make the obligations to them the same as those to other protected classes. Persons with disabilities gain the same benefits of laws prohibiting discrimination on the basis of race, color, religion, national origin, or sex.

State nondiscrimination laws may also cover places of public accommodation, which in the housing area means inns, hotels, motels.

State nondiscrimination laws, while enumerating prohibited practices usually do not specify the standard of accessibility to be addressed in the housing units. However, as a practical matter state human rights agencies look to the provisions of the state building code, particularly provisions in the architectural barrier section (or in the state architectural barrier law, if separate) for the standard of access. These are cited in Appendix I.

There are other noteworthy features about state laws. Generally they do not mandate that an owner make changes to make a structure or unit accessible, if the unit met the state code when built. Also, the state law will not require each unit to be fully accessible. The units to be accessible will be specified by a fixed number or as a specified percentage of the total. The precise number varies and each jurisdiction needs to be checked.

State laws provide for alternative methods of enforcement through the state administrative agency, usually the civil or human rights office, or directly in the courts in actions brought by the alleged victim. The range of methods follows the same pattern as extended under the employment laws, which is really not surprising since the housing and public accommodations provisions are usually additional sections in the basic law of the state that prohibits discrimination. The range of remedies under the state laws may include injunctions prohibiting further discriminatory conduct, an order directing the sale or rental of comparable facilities, damages and attorney's fees.

Many states have "White Cane" laws which provide that persons who are visually handicapped or have other physical disabilities shall have full and equal access to housing accommodations offered for rent, lease, or compensation subject to all applicable conditions as would be any member of the general public. These are found in express provisions relating to housing or in the provisions related to places of public accommodations. Enforcement of these laws is vested in the state attorney general as the offense is being a crime, commonly a misdemeanor.

White Cane laws embody public policy. Recipients of federal aid and non-federally assisted housing providers should not view them as hortatory language.

White Cane laws are customarily limited to protecting only persons who are physically disabled, as is the case in the District of Columbia, Delaware, and Iowa. States such as Missouri and New York limit the protections to persons who are blind or who are deaf and do not protect, in the White Cane law, persons with other impairments such as those who are mobility impaired.

The White Cane law may apply in conjunction with other nondiscrimination provisions, such as in Maryland, the District of Columbia or New York, or even in jurisdictions such as Georgia where state civil rights law does not afford protection in housing or places of public accommodation to persons with disabilities (see Appendix I).

Finally, state laws are critical in housing because when the issue is new construction or rehabilitation, the state building codes come into effect. Whether enforced by the state or local jurisdiction, such as a municipality or a county, there are defined times at which access is required to be checked. To avoid problems later, accessibility should be ensured at the time plans are approved and the building permit issued, as well as when the certificate of occupancy is issued after construction is completed. State laws are also significant because tax benefits may be available for accessible housing for either new or used units, as is the case in North Carolina. Deductions and exemptions from taxes are available in a few other states, such as Nevada and Arizona.

Adaptable/Accessible Housing

In the area of housing for persons with disabilities, the most recent technical provisions relating to accessible and adaptable housing are most significant. This is because adaptability and accessibility clearly recognize the emergence of the notion of universal design, i.e., what benefits "disabled" persons really can benefit everyone. A grade level entrance, reinforced walls, switches and controls at appropriate heights, while clearly usable for an non-disabled person, can also be functional for a person with disabilities, thus maximizing the marketing potential of the unit. Adaptable housing draws from the concept of universality of functional design. Adaptable housing is an integral part of the accessibility requirements under the HUD 504 and Fair Housing Act Amendments of 1988 regulations.

The standards for accessibility are relatively recent. The original ANSI A117.1 was issued in 1961. It was not until it was revised in 1980 that it contained provisions related to dwelling units and residential structures. ANSI A117.1 was reissued with minor revisions in 1986. It is due to be reviewed and reissued in 1991.

The federal government, which for years had had numerous rules affecting persons with disabilities, did not achieve a detailed, express standard in accessible housing until it adopted the UFAS in 1984.

Meanwhile, the notion gaining acceptance was that dwellings could be designed so that the unit would be usable now by a "non-disabled" person and later converted or adapted for a person with disabilities. Walls that were reinforced in the construction of a unit could later have grab bars added to them. Staircases that were wide enough could later have chairlifts added if the user was unable to go up and down the stairs independently. An apartment house could be converted into a nursing home at a significantly lower cost if the units had access potential.

That potential is increasing as in more instances the 1980 ANSI and UFAS are applied. In designing and building dwelling units it is now much easier to achieve accessibility by complying with delineated requirements. (By contrast, the original ANSI had nothing explicit on dwelling units.) Having accessibility and adaptability of dwelling units as an integral part of the standards, both public (UFAS) and private (ANSI), makes creating adaptable units easier as the particular considerations for the units are noted right in the standards, providing true guidance for those affected.

Fortunately, both the private and the public sectors have had the good sense of incorporating their technical provisions related to accessibility and adaptability of dwelling units in the same numbered section: 4.3.4. ANSI 1980 and UFAS contain virtually identical provisions related to dwelling units.

Set forth below is a series of items to be checked. Weigh them and use them to assess the adaptability or the accessibility of a particular unit, whether free standing as a separate home or as a part of a large complex. This checklist is based on UFAS. A final caveat: the list is not a substitute for state/local/federal requirements. Rather it is provided to enable the user of the list to assess the particular unit and elements within the bigger facility in functional terms.

In Appendix I the technical standards for accessibility in each state are specified. Here are the several features, in and around a unit, which must be checked in order to make that unit immediately accessible or adaptable so future users with disabilities can function within it. Check the items listed against the requirements of those applicable noted in Appendix I.

Adaptability/Accessibility Functionality Checklist

1. Space allowances—within all rooms and spaces.
2. Accessible routes—within the dwelling unit to all rooms and spaces; connecting the accessible/adaptable dwelling unit to common use areas/facilities; to public transit/parking/public streets; to accessible facilities/structures on a

common site; to accessible entrances; to the accessible
spaces and features within the building or complex.

3. Floor surfaces – all rooms, spaces, and routes.
4. Parking/passenger loading areas – if provided for non-dis-
    abled persons.
5. Windows – if operable.
6. Doors – at the entrance to the unit, the building, and spaces.
7. Entrance – including communication devices to announce
    visitors, doorbells, telephones, and the door.
8. Storage – if provided for non-disabled persons.
9. Controls – heating, air-conditioning, lighting, etc.
10. Emergency alarms – audio/visual and set at frequencies
    which will not cause problems for other groups, such as
    persons with seizure disorders.
11. Bathrooms – lavatories, water closets, sinks, mirrors,
    tubs/showers if provided, storage areas.
12. Kitchens – all areas including food serving, cooking, prepara-
    tion, cleaning functions.
13. Laundry facilities – if provided, whether within a unit or in a
    common area.
14. Common use areas and facilities - to the extent provided for
    non-disabled persons including employment opportunities
    in large housing areas.
15. Patios/terraces, balconies, carports, garages – provided with
    the unit, whether on site or nearby.

More Practical Points

The preceding checklist has the technical items. It is also
essential to know which and how many units must be accessible.
Those are questions to be addressed with care because of the
complexity of the rules.

Here are some additional practical points that may help address that and other thorny issues:

1. Keep in mind that the unit will be used by more than the
    first group of users. Plan for future generations.

2. Consider that a person with a disability wants and will pay for the same functionality, use, convenience, and independence in housing as a person who is not disabled.

3. Consult legal counsel as well as architects/designers conversant with accessible/adaptable housing to be sure you are complying with the rules.

4. The rights and obligations related to persons with disabilities, especially as applied to persons with physical disabilities, as far as state/local housing are concerned, are generally the same as those affecting minorities, women, and other classes afforded protection.

5. If there is a conflict between standards, whether federal, state, or local, a safe operating rule is to follow the standard which results in the most accessibility.

6. Pay particular attention to common areas as well as first floor units.

7. Keep in mind all funding sources and that each has undoubtedly conditioned funding on certain requirements.

8. Check for local housing incentive programs, including those for elderly persons, and see how that can be dovetailed.

9. Check with persons with disabilities in the community as well as their advocacy organizations for persons interested in an accessible or adaptable unit.

10. Check for tax incentives for renovations, especially in business properties.

11. Remember to check for specific requirements but start from the notion of at least 5 percent (minimum one) of each type of unit is to be accessible. Ground floor units, too, should and easily can be accessible.

12. AFTER the decision has been made to provide housing for the user with a disability it is perfectly allowable to discuss what must be done for the particular person. That person will know what is most functional for them.

A Final Note

Accessible and adaptable housing are the most dynamic features in the development of housing standards. This will be of increasing practical importance as more persons with disabilities become consumers of housing The graying of our population, with the vast increase in the number of senior citizens projected as the "baby boomers" age, will only accelerate the demand for accessible or adaptable housing. Since it is functional, universal design, one can only wonder what took it so long to get here.

Chapter 5

EDUCATION

Introduction

In the 1960s civil rights movement we often heard the refrain, "Burn, baby, burn." As those of us who participated in that movement had our own children and settled into our niches, a more appropriate mantra for us would have been to implore them to "Learn, baby, learn."

When my children started attending schools I was fortunate enough to be able to walk with them around the corner from our home to the local elementary school. As neighborhood demographics changed, the kids began riding those familiar yellow school buses, riding for almost an hour to what seemed a totally new world. When I mentioned the long ride and new environment to a friend who has a child with a disability, his response was, "Welcome to my world, but at least we have status."

My friend was right. Under section 504 of the Rehabilitation Act as well as the Education for All Handicapped Children Act (EAHCA), P.L. 94-142, renamed in 1990 the Individuals with Disabilities Education Act (IDEA), P.L. 101-476, parents of disabled children do have basic rights or "status." These are rights to a free appropriate public education which includes, substantially, proper evaluations, testing, placements, courses with support and educationally related services, and procedural safeguards including notices of changes, annual individual educational programs, and impartial hearing rights.

The Individuals with Disabilities Education Act is not the only critical law here. Section 504 of the Rehabilitation Act, with its mandate not to discriminate against qualified handicapped individuals, has a major role, particularly at the post-secondary level. Both statutes are crucial because of the significant amount of federal funds provided for education to state and local school authorities. Education program receiving federal funds may not discriminate against qualified persons with disabilities. The Americans with Disabilities Act enacted in 1990 is also of import to public and private educational entities, which under Titles I, II, and III, may not discriminate against qualified individuals with disabilities in their programs, activities, services, and employment practices.

It must be noted that the rights for disabled children that are presently articulated in the statutes were originally recognized judicially as having a constitutional basis. The court cases recognized that administrative mismanagement and consequent financial difficulties did not excuse not serving disabled children, a principle which loomed of increasing import as federal, state, and local governments encountered fiscal problems in the 1990s. Those early landmark decisions established a pattern of the courts playing an especially significant role in determining the qualification of persons for programs, the nature and quality of the education and services to be provided, as well as employability of persons with disabilities in educational institutions.

The objective of this chapter is to provide readers a basic understanding of what is required under the law, so that concepts can be grasped and applied, eliminating unnecessary confrontations. A sample policy statement implementing EAHCA as well as a policy statement on procedural rights under EAHCA are found at the end of this chapter along with a chart illustrating the continuum of educational placements available.

Application Of The Rehabilitation Act

Section 504 of the Rehabilitation Act prohibits discrimination in programs or activities receiving federal financial assistance. This has direct application in the education field since all states receive federal education money. Usually this is funding provided by the Department of Education, though other federal agencies may also provide assistance. While the states may, in turn, make subgrants of those funds to local school districts, this serves only to extend the federal mandate to that local level.

Section 504 applies to persons who are physically or mentally disabled, have a record of such an impairment, or who are regarded as having an impairment. When the Americans with Disabilities Act was enacted in 1990, this definition was amended for purposes of programs and activities providing education to exclude any individual who currently uses illegal drugs when a covered entity acts on the basis of such drug use. Former drug users, individuals in supervised drug rehabilitation programs, and persons erroneously regarded as engaging in drug use, are covered and protected by the Rehabilitation Act.

Section 504 has the same broad sweep as other civil rights laws applicable in the education field. Its coverage extends to program services, to facilities, and to employment.

It should be kept in mind that the initial regulations issued by the federal government to implement section 504 were those of the then Department of Health, Education, and Welfare. Those rules were later reissued by the Department of Education when it was created shortly thereafter.

The regulations established the pattern of federal rules under section 504. There are general prohibitions against discrimination in a program or activity receiving assistance. In the employment area, discrimination is prohibited and reasonable accommodation to the known physical or mental limitations of otherwise qualified handicapped applicants or employees is required. Employment criteria, including testing, must not discriminate and pre-employment medical examinations or inquiries are limited to job-related functions and may not go to whether a person is handicapped or the severity of the disability (see Chapter 2). Program accessibility in structures required that new structures as well as alterations had to meet the technical accessibility code (originally ANSI A117.1-1961(r.1971) now the Uniform Federal Accessibility Standard ("UFAS"). This meant that by 1980 campuses and school districts receiving federal aid had to have their programs available to qualified handicapped persons. It meant the entire program had to be offered in an accessible site, not that the entire site had to be fully accessible. While access was required in new facilities, older facilities were required to be modified only to the extent necessary to ensure that the services were available. Conceivably, as with other service areas, an entire education program could be made available on the first floor and it would not be necessary to put in an elevator to access the other floors. On the other hand, institutions cannot band together to form a consortium and offer accessible courses in only one of them. If colleges share programs with other institutions, each part of the program, wherever situated, must be accessible. Neighboring schools cannot trade programs amongst them, e.g., one making its liberal arts programs accessible and the other making the engineering programs accessible. If each school receives federal funds then each school must have each of its offerings program accessible. Structural modifications to existing facilities are not required if alternative means of providing the services are available, a principle reiterated in the Civil Rights Restoration Act of 1988 ("CRRA"). For example, rather than modify the structure containing the program such as by putting in an elevator to a top floor of a multi-story building, the services may be made effectively available by relocating the program to the accessible site, i.e., another classroom on the ground floor. Carrying a person is an unacceptable method of achieving program accessibility. It is dangerous, as well as embarrassing to the individuals involved.

The regulations elaborate on the meaning of section 504 in preschool, elementary, secondary, adult and private educational programs which receive federal financial assistance. Qualified handicapped persons, regardless of the severity of their physical or mental disability (as a practical matter, virtually all handicapped children), are to receive a free, appropriate public education. This may mean that the recipient will have to pay for private schools if the appropriate educational services are unavailable in its program. Recipients were to provide not only the strictly traditional academic educational services but also counseling, extracurricular activities, physical education, health, and transportation services necessary for handicapped students to be afforded equal opportunity to participate.

The regulations recognize the importance of the educational setting and state a strong preference for education in an academic setting; evaluation and placement procedures are set forth. Recipients are required to maintain procedural safeguards for the identification, evaluation, placement and provision of services for persons who believe they are qualified.

In the area of post-secondary including vocational education, the regulations elaborate upon the precepts that admission and recruitment practices must be nondiscriminatory, as must be the treatment of students. Academic adjustments may have to be made in the program, including time for completing the degree, substitution of certain courses, and in the taking of examinations. Auxiliary aids, such as taped materials and sign language interpreters, are some of the special services that must be provided. Housing must be provided for disabled students that is comparable, convenient, accessible and at the same cost as to others. Financial and employment opportunities must be provided to the same extent that they are provided to students who are not disabled. There is also the mandate to provide nonacademic services, such as counseling and physical education, to handicapped persons.

The concept of who is a qualified handicapped individual is a crucial one. The case of *Davis v. Southeastern Community College*, 442 U.S.397 (1979), was a pivotal, unanimous decision of the United States Supreme Court which first construed section 504.

In upholding the college's refusal to admit Mrs. Davis, a deaf woman, into a program which would have led her to becoming a registered nurse, the Court held that the college could consider legitimate physical requirements during its admission process. Colleges did not have to make "major adjustments" to programs to accommodate handicapped students. Section 504 required that programs be administered in a nondiscriminatory manner. It did not require affirmative action by recipients. Mrs. Davis' hearing impairment was so severe that she would have been unable to undertake a fundamental part of the course.

Disabled persons have sought, and been recognized as qualified, to teach in educational settings. There have been a series of cases involving this concept as persons with disabilities moved into the mainstream. This trend began with a teacher who is blind and extended in the mid-1980s to a teacher with tuberculosis.

In the mid-1980s there were several court cases involving children with Acquired Immunity Deficiency Syndrome (AIDS), all of whom wound up in class with non-AIDS students for periods of time as their health permitted. Consequently, school systems began to develop policies to guide their interactions with students and faculty with AIDS. See, Appendix III. The United States Department of Education recognizes persons with AIDS as covered by the Rehabilitation Act.

Another significant line of decisions involving persons with disabilities in what, before the enactment of the laws, would have been thought to be, at best, a nontraditional role, relates to young athletes who had disabilities seeking to participate in intercollegiate and interscholastic athletics. These cases involve examination of what it means to be qualified and the documented risks to the individual and to other participants. These are judgment questions where the facts and expert testimony are critical to the decision. Students who may have lost an organ or limb but who are otherwise qualified may not be excluded by recipients from contact sports. However, such students may be required to obtain parental consent as well as approval for participation from the doctor most familiar with their condition. If the school system provides its athletes with medical care insurance for sickness or accident, it must make the insurance available for athletes with disabilities. Schools are not required to establish intramural athletic programs to accommodate disabled students who are unable to compete with non-disabled students in interscholastic sports.

In discussing the mandate of section 504 it must be kept in mind that as a result of the Civil Rights Restoration Act of 1988 ("CRRA") the mandate not to discriminate under the federal law is not limited to the program specifically receiving the federal aid. The nondiscrimination mandate now extends generally to all of a recipient's programs and activities if the recipient of federal aid is a department, agency, special purpose district (including, for example, a school district) or other instrumentality of state and local government, college, university, or public system of higher education, an elementary or secondary school system. If the recipient of federal aid is a corporation which provides educational services, the federal nondiscrimination mandate applies to the entire corporation. CRRA reversed *Grove City v. Bell*, 465 U.S.555 (1984), a Supreme Court decision which had limited federal civil rights mandates to the specific program receiving the aid, in contrast to all activities and programs of the recipients of federal aid.

It is important to observe that several states have laws prohibiting discrimination in education against disabled persons. These are noted in Appendix I. These laws are often limited in their scope of application to specified levels of education, such as post-secondary. Also, in some states educational facilities and programs may be within the mandate not to discriminate in places of public accommodation.

Individuals With Disabilities Education Act
(Education For All Handicapped Children Act)

Returning to the federal law, the particularity of a funding statute is embodied in the Education for All Handicapped Children Act (EAHCA), renamed in 1990 by P.L. 101-476 the Individuals with Disabilities Education Act (IDEA). This is a substantive education law, not a civil rights statute, which states implement with state laws and regulations. It is a federal funding for program services statute.

Readers are advised that much of the discussion here, as well as in other literature and the cases, speaks in terms of EAHCA and handicapped children, not IDEA. This is because the education programs, policies and cases evolved under EAHCA which is written in terms of "handicapped" children.

The IDEA (EAHCA) requires handicapped children receive a free appropriate public education. This special education will be at public expense in the least restrictive environment and will include the provision of appropriate related services. Procedural safeguards must be established to ensure an impartial due process to resolve disputes. All of the states, under the law, must identify and evaluate students in need of special education.

The initial inquiry is who gets served. As originally enacted, the law was to fund programs for children from 3 to 21 years of age, with each state having discretion to fund children under 5 and over 18, except if state law required funding of children ages 3–5 or 18-21. In 1986, in the Handicapped Children's Protection Act, P.L. 99-457, preschool children ages 3–5, were phased into coverage. The 1986 law provides incentives for states to fund handicapped children ages 3–5. If a state does not do so, it could lose other federal funds. The 1986 law also added Subpart H to EAHCA, a discretionary program for children from birth to age two.

Those who will benefit from special education are children who are mentally retarded, hard of hearing, deaf, visually handicapped, seriously emotionally disturbed, orthopedically impaired, children with specific learning disabilities (e.g., dyslexia), autism, traumatic brain injury as well as children with other health impairments. A very significant decision of a federal court of appeals in 1989, *Timothy W. v. Rochester, New Hampshire*, 875 F. 2d 954 (1st. Cir. 1989), upheld the "zero-reject" principle of EAHCA, namely that all children regardless of the extent of their disability, who were otherwise eligible, had to receive special education services. In this case the school district was required to provide a free appropriate public education to a child whose multiple disabilities included mental retardation, cerebral palsy and quadriplegia. The court rejected the school district's claim that the child was ineligible since he could not benefit from special education services.

Eligible children are entitled to a free appropriate public education, which means special education and related services provided at public expense, under public supervision and direction, meeting the standards of the state agency, including an appropriate education agency of the state and in conformity with the Individual Education Program (IEP).

An appropriate education must be measured against the individual needs of the child. The child needs to obtain the special education and related services that will enable the child to benefit from the instruction. This is not a guarantee of success or the chance for the "best" education. "Appropriate" does not translate into "best" legally. Rather, it means the "floor of opportunity" to succeed.

The concept of the EAHCA is that the child gets all the traditional educational services—reading, language arts, etc.—as well as the necessary related services. The notion of related services under EAHCA is similar to that addressed under the Rehab Act, section 504. Under EAHCA, related services will include such services as speech, audiology, counseling, occupational therapy, physical therapy, psychological, health, and transportation services that the particular child needs. In 1990 when extending the EAHCA for five years and renaming it the

Individuals with Disabilities Education Act, P.L. 101-476, Congress made clear that social work and rehabilitation services also were to be considered related services to which eligible disabled children were entitled, if appropriate. Not all children get all services; each child receives only those services which are appropriate for it to have for the particular school year. An Individual Education Program "IEP" of academic program and related services is prepared annually, commonly with periodic reviews throughout the school year.

The 1990 law added the requirement that the IEP of eligible students, no later than age 16, provide for transition services to enable the student to move from school to post-school activities.

Three areas have been of special concern: health services, transportation services, and disciplining disabled students.

In the health area it is now clear that for the services to be required the child must be so handicapped as to require special education; the service must be necessary to aid the child in gaining benefits from the special education provided and the services must be provided, not by a physician, but by a nurse or other qualified person. Medical equipment is not to be provided. Health services may include clean intermittent catheterization.

Handicapped children commonly receive transportation to schools. The site of the school is to be the appropriate one, not necessarily the school nearest the child's home. The issue of transportation is often linked with the question of the appropriateness of the placement, as long journeys on school buses are generally frowned upon for educational purposes.

The third issue, disciplining disabled students, is enmeshed with the procedural provisions and safeguards of the EAHCA affecting the child's placement and program.

The placement of the child is to be in the least restrictive alternative environment. This is a recognition that it may be necessary to provide children with special services but is a basically integrationist philosophy. It is a reaction in law to the fact that prior to the EAHCA many disabled children were shunted aside, kept in separate facilities and did not receive anything close to the education others received. Congress was seeking to enable all children to benefit from interacting with each other. The practice is that school systems develop a number of placement levels, ranging from a child obtaining some special education services in the regular classroom to a child with severe difficulties being placed in a residential setting. The chart at the end of this chapter illustrates these diverse levels. Note that for the first three levels the child is in school with all the children who are not disabled. At first the child is receiving some special services in his classroom. This is "mainstreaming." The fourth level is a special class for the entire school day, though the entire class is within the mainstream or regular school building. Beyond that we begin to see special schools for particularly difficult cases. In determining what is the least restrictive alternative environment it is important to ascertain what progress is being made. Decision-makers must examine closely the totality of each particular child's needs. It is not acceptable under the concept of least restrictive environment for all children to be automatically placed in one facility, even if that place is the so-called mainstream classroom.

If a school system does not offer the appropriate program it can reimburse a private provider of such services. Most recently, school systems have been moving to expand the range of services offered, thereby seeking to retain more children within their system and avoid the expenses of tuition, transportation, and other necessarily related costs entailed in the non-public school placement.

The Act contains detailed procedural safeguards. An illustrative implementation of those safeguards by a local education agency is set out at the end of this chapter. Parents receive notice of the development of the IEP and may participate in that process. They are notified of all changes in it and are given notice of their right to a hearing if they disagree with either the placement or the services the school system proposes to provide their child.

The underlying rationale here is to keep the focus on the child and to ensure the appropriateness of the education and benefits to the child. Thus, a disagreement by either parent with the school system can lead to reconsideration of the IEP or invocation of the due process hearing process. This situation arises more frequently now with the increasing number of divorced parents. The key here is the child, not the parents.

There can be a public hearing before an official designated by the local school agency to hear and decide the case. At the hearing both sides present evidence about the child and the child's need for special education and related services. It is common for expert consultants and attorneys to participate for both the parents and the school district. The decision is issued shortly thereafter (within 30 days) and may be appealed for a full new hearing to the state education agency and from there to federal court. While the hearing process is ongoing the child remains, as a general rule, in the present placement. This provision is known as the "Stay Put" rule.

The "Stay Put" rule also has been recognized as prohibiting school systems from disciplining (expelling or suspending) a student for disability related behavior for more than ten (10) days without a hearing and other procedural protections of EAHCA. That was the holding by the United States Supreme Court in *Honig v. Doe*, 484 U.S. 305 (1988), it has also been recognized that a series of suspensions that are each 10 days or fewer in duration creates a pattern of exclusions can constitute a significant change of placement. This also triggers the procedural protections of EAHCA, including the "Stay Put" rule. The Americans with Disabilities Act made clear that a school district could discipline a disabled student who uses drugs or alcohol to the same extent it could discipline a nondisabled student. In such a situation the special EAHCA protections, including "Stay Put," would not apply.

The concept of "free" appropriate public education must be kept in mind here, too. As noted previously, a school system will have to pay for a non-public placement if that is appropriate for the particular child and the system does not offer such appropriate educational and related services. It has been held that school authorities had to reimburse costs of private special education if that placement was ultimately found to be the appropriate one for the child. This is true even if the parents had placed the child, unilaterally that is, without the consent of the school system while the legal process was working itself out.

Another financial consideration that changed in 1986 was that of the expenses of attorneys and expert consultants. As a result of the Handicapped Children's Protection Act those expenses are now recoupable by a parent who is successful at either the hearing before the state or local agency or in court. This legislation had the effect of overturning a decision of the United States Supreme Court which had held that attorney's fees were not reimbursable under EAHCA. There have even been cases where attorney's fees have been awarded after court settlement of EAHCA litigation in which the child has obtained the placement sought by agreement and not pursuant to a court finding. In the 1990 Individuals with Disabilities Education Act, P.L. 101-476, Congress made clear that states could not claim they were immune from suit under EAHCA due to sovereign immunity stemming from the eleventh amendment of the United States Constitution.

Finally, it should be observed that, as a practical matter, many persons tend to blur the distinction between the EAHCA and section 504. When both apply, the courts defer to EAHCA. It is much more specific and is a funding statute with more narrow application. In October, 1988, the United States Department of Education made clear that there are differences in the two statutes and their implementing regulation, each of which must be complied with independently of the other. However the Department of Education also made clear that compliance with EAHCA was one way recipients could meet their 504 obligations.

At the end if this chapter are examples of implementation of EAHCA by local education agencies. A general policy statement, the chart on the continuum of services, and a statement of procedural safeguards are included. All of these are models which can be modified and adapted by local educational agencies. AIDS related education materials are in Appendix III.

Americans with Disabilities Act (ADA)

The ADA, discussed at greater length in Chapters 2 and 3, also applies to educational institutions, programs and activities, both public and (nonreligious) private. State and local governments (including state and local educational districts and other entities) are subject to the mandate of Title II not to discriminate in provision of public services. Private schools are places of public accommodation in Title III of ADA. Employment discrimination against qualified individuals with disabilities is prohibited in both the private and public educational sectors. State and local public schools are thus subject to ADA rules from the United States Equal Employment Opportunity Commission (Title I–employment) and the United States Department of Justice (Title II–state and local government services). Private educational entities are also subject to several ADA rules, including those of the United States Equal Employment Opportunity Commission (Title I–employment), United States Department of Justice (Title III–public accommodations) and, as seen in Chapter 6, the United States Department of Transportation (Title III–transit services). All of these ADA rules were required to be finalized by July 26, 1991, one year after enactment of the ADA.

ADA also requires that any person who offers courses/examinations for secondary or post-secondary education, professional or trade purposes offer such courses/examinations in a manner and place accessible to persons with disabilities or make alternative accessible arrangements.

A Final Note

The process of education is said to be one of growth by drawing from within. The EAHCA, now IDEA, and Rehab Act embrace that philosophy by seeking wherever practical and appropriate to draw students who are disabled and non-disabled, teachers, and administrators together. Accommodations and related services, as necessary, are to be provided on an individualized basis.

The benefits of these laws transcend the particular programs which are funded and executed. When people are brought together for educational purposes they learn more than the academic curricula. They also learn about people. And, given the long history of excluding persons with disabilities from the public education system, the value of people learning about people must not be underestimated.

POLICY BOARD OF EDUCATION OF MONTGOMERY COUNTY   IOB

Related Entries: EHA, IGC-RA, IGC-RB, IOC, IOC-RA

Education of Handicapped Children

A. Purpose

Montgomery County Public Schools is committed to the education of all handicapped children to prepare them, to the maximum extent possible, for self-sufficient and productive lives as full participating members of our society. This policy establishes guidelines for working toward these objectives, and for all necessary activities to comply with Federal and State mandates.

The Board reiterates its commitment to the *Goals of Education* and acknowledges that the development of effective programs for all students depends not only upon adequate budgetary provisions, but also upon the energy, concern, and leadership demonstrated at all levels.

The Board recognizes that attitudinal and physical barriers must be overcome and that adequate supports must be provided so that handicapped children can be educated in the most natural and integrated setting possible. The responsibility for effective programs must be shared by both general and special education personnel.

The Board recognizes that education of handicapped children is complex and necessitates cooperation with other state and local public agencies and private service providers to provide a full continuum and range of services for these students.

The Board recognizes the importance and value of family involvement in the education of handicapped students, including participation in individual program planning, and the importance of assuring the rights of parents and students to due process and confidentiality of records.

B. Process and Content

Provisions for educating handicapped children shall include:

1. Free and appropriate educational programs and related services
These appropriate services will be available to children from birth through age 20. Programs and services will be provided on the same level of intensity and will be of the same quality level as for all other children in MCPS. They are to begin as soon as the child can benefit from them. For children under

the age of five, these services will be phased in according to legally mandated timeliness.

2. Comprehensive Annual Plan
   There will be a comprehensive annual plan for identification and delivery of services and programs to handicapped children. The plan will be reviewed by appropriate advisory groups and at public hearings. There will be opportunity for public comment, consistent with MCPS procedures for policy adoption before submission to the state superintendent of schools. The plan will include provisions for supervision and monitoring of programs and services, and for at least annual review of each child's program.

3. Identification
   There will be an ongoing and systematic effort to identify all handicapped children who may be in need of special education services.

4. Evaluation
   Appropriate educational and other assessments will be conducted to determine whether a child is in need of special education services and to develop an individualized education program for each handicapped child.
   a. Assessment instruments will be appropriately adapted to the child's handicapping conditions, age, socio-economic and cultural background.
   b. Assessment will be administered in the child's primary language.
   c. Interpreters will be provided in the child's primary language, when necessary, throughout all phases of the evaluation process.
   d. No single assessment result will be used to determine placement.
   e. Written and informed parental consent will be obtained before a child suspected of being handicapped will be evaluated.
   f. Parents may, at their own expense, initiate assessment of the child which may be used to consider program options.
   g. Evaluation and reevaluation will take place within the legally prescribed time period. Reevaluations will be conducted sooner than legally specified, if necessary.
   h. Private and parochial school students suspected of being handicapped will also be evaluated at no cost to the parent at sites designated by MCPS.

5. Multidisciplinary Teams
   Each school will have at least one educational management
   team, chaired by an administrator. Team members will form
   the nucleus for admission, review, and dismissal (ARD)
   teams. ARD teams will include specialists appropriate for the
   child's handicapping condition. They will review assessment information, determine whether a handicapping condition exists,
   and make placement recommendations.

6. Individualized Education Programs (IEP)
   Each handicapped child will have a written IEP, encompassing
   strengths, needs, program assignment, percent of time in a
   regular program, goals, objectives and timeliness for reviewing
   progress. Plans will include services needed but unavailable.
   Plans will be developed jointly by parents, teacher(s),
   specialists responsible for the implementation of the IEP, and
   an administrator. Parents or staff members may invite other
   persons to participate in the IEP development. Pertinent information about teaching strategies and materials will be included in the plan. Supervisory personnel will periodically
   review IEPs to monitor general plan development and implementation.

7. Parent Involvement
   Parents or guardians of handicapped children will be en-
   couraged to participate in all educational decision-making.
   They will be invited to ARD meetings scheduled, whenever
   possible, to permit parents to participate. Funds will be made
   available to provide for such meetings outside of regular work
   hours including the summer.

   Parents or guardians will be informed of procedures for obtaining informed parental consent before evaluation and placement of children and for parent or guardian participation in
   the IEP review process.

   Parents or guardians have the right to inspect, review, copy,
   and challenge any educational records relating to their
   children and to be advised of the types and locations of such
   records. Staff will be prepared to help parents or guardians understand the records. If needed, staff will receive additional
   training to be prepared to respond to parental requests for
   such help.

8. Continuum of Educational Services
   A continuum of educational services will be provided so that
   students can be placed in public or private programs appropriate to their individual needs, considering intensity of services, instructional adaptations, and specialized services.

Instruction of handicapped students will follow the regular
MCPS *Program of Studies*, adapted to accommodate student
learning styles where necessary. Appropriate curricula and special education instructional materials will be developed and
maintained.

9. Placement
   Handicapped children will be placed in the most enabling instructional environment to accomplish the goals of the IEP.
   They will be given a chance to go to school in the most natural
   and integrated setting that is appropriate, i.e., whenever possible, in regular school settings with nonhandicapped children
   of the same age group.

   a. Least Restrictive Environment—Mainstreaming
      When students can profit from full-time, part-time or oc-
      casional participation in the regular program, schools are
      expected to make reasonable accommodations to the
      specific needs of the handicapped child to promote ap-
      propriate integration.

   b. Non-MCPS Programs
      When a child is placed in a non-MCPS setting, in accord-
      ance with Maryland State Department of Education Re-
      quirements, MCPS personnel will monitor the program
      delivered to the child to assure that participating schools
      meet MCPS program standards.

10. Vocational and Career Educational Programs
    Vocational and career education programs designed or
    adapted for handicapped children will be made available. They
    will include those activities needed to prepare the child for
    self-sufficient and productive living as an adult. Staff will
    make a concerted effort to ensure that available program op-
    tions will be adequate.

11. Staffing Ratios
    Student/staff ratios will be commensurate with the needs of
    the different levels of service provided. The Board of Educa-
    tion supports staffing ratios that are appropriate to the in-
    dividualized needs of children, to the extent feasible, even if
    they are smaller than maximum staffing ratios permitted by
    the MSDE.

12. Extracurricular Activities
    Handicapped students will have an opportunity to participate
    in appropriate extracurricular activities that are generally avail-
    able to all MCPS students in the community. Together with
    other community agencies, MCPS will continue to develop spe-

cialized extracurricular activities when regularly provided extracurricular programs do not meet existing needs.

13. Transportation
MCPS or privately contracted transportation will be provided so that handicapped children can be moved to and from school in a reasonable time. The special needs of the handicapped child will be taken into account when planning for transportation needs.

14. Staff Development
   a. General Education
      In-service training programs will be developed so that general educators can acquire a basic understanding of handicapped children and their families and can learn to work effectively with the handicapped.

   b. Special Education
      Special education personnel must keep informed of changes produced by technological improvement and of new educational strategies and materials resulting from research and demonstration activities. Opportunities for continuing professional development based on identified individual or group staff needs will be provided.

15. Increased Student Awareness of Handicapped
Programs will be developed to increase the understanding of the handicapped among the student body of MCPS and to provide mutually beneficial interaction between handicapped and nonhandicapped students. Planning will be done cooperatively with other MCPS offices, community agencies, parents and students.

16. Confidentiality of Student Records
Information about a handicapped student will be collected and used in such a way that the confidentiality of the information is insured and the student's right to privacy is guaranteed.

17. Procedural safeguards will be maintained to guarantee due process for children, parents, and staff when there are disagreements about educational decisions.

C. Review and Reporting

   1. The superintendent will report specific progress on the implementation and monitoring of this policy to the Board of Education at least annually, or more frequently, as directed by the Board of Education. These reports shall include views of parent/community representatives.

   2. The Office of Special and Alternative Education will collaborate with the Department of Educational Accountability for internal and external data collection/analysis and evalua-

tion activities and will report findings to the superintendent and the Board of Education.

3. The comprehensive plan for services and programs for the handicapped will be updated annually, revised as needed, and reported to the Board of Education and the Maryland State Department of Education. Budget implications will be reported to the Board of Education, as appropriate.

4. All regulations developed in support of this policy will be sent to the board as information items.

Resolution No. 834-78, December 5, 1978 (directory information updated) reaffirmed by Resolution No. 19-85, January 8, 1985, reformatted in accordance with Resolution 333-86, June 12, 1986, and Resolution 458-86, August 12, 1986.

The MCPS Continuum of Services

The graphic illustrates that the needs of most MCPS students are met at Level 1 of the Continuum. The intensity of services increases from Level 1 through Level 6. The number of students requiring more services decreases. Related services for students needing special education are available at all levels of the continuum.

Level 6— Residential Education and services for the severely handicapped.

Level 5—Special school or location in a regular school. Program provided for the entire day.

Level 4—Special Class. Program provided up to six hours a day in a special education classroom in a regular public school building. Students participate in regular education programs when appropriate.

Level 3—Resource Room. Students receive most of their program in the regular classroom, but may receive up to three hours of daily supplementary special education services in a resource room. Specialists consult, plan, and assist regular classroom teachers to deliver the individual education program each student needs.

Level 2—Itinerant Service. Students in regular classrooms may receive up to one hour daily of supplementary instruction or service from a specialist. These may include counseling services, auditory, vision, speech/language assistance, or physical/occupational therapy.

Level 1—Teacher consultation. This support is provided to a regular classroom teacher to enable the teacher to assist a student with special needs. These services to staff may include observations, assessments, conferences, or specific information on teaching or dealing with student behaviors.

fewer ↑   *number of students* ↓   *more*

more ↑   *intensity of need* ↓   *less*

Fairfax County Public Schools
Department of Student Services and Special Education
Fairfax, Virginia

Procedural Safeguards and Due Process Provisions for Handicapped Children in the Fairfax County Public Schools

All resident handicapped children, ages two through twenty-one, are entitled to a free, appropriate public education. Free, appropriate public education means special education and related services which are provided at public expense, under public supervision and direction, and without charge; meet the standards of the state educational agency; include preschool, elementary school, secondary school, or vocational education; make available physical education; are provided in conformity with an individualized education program; and are provided in the least restrictive environment. The school system provides a continuum of placements to meet the needs of handicapped students. Written parental consent must be obtained prior to evaluation or any change in identification or placement of handicapped children. Such consent is voluntary and may be revoked at any time.

The following procedural safeguards and due process provisions have been incorporated into the specific guidelines for general education screening, eligibility, placement and dismissal procedures for special education programs. These are contained in Fairfax County Public Schools Regulation 3401.1P.

I. Referral/Local Screening

Permission for Testing
If there is reason to believe that your child is in need of special education services, or if your child is currently receiving special education services and requires reevaluation, referral will be made to the school's local screening committee. You may request testing by addressing your request, in writing, to the principal. The principal will notify you within ten working days of the local screening committee decision regarding the request to evaluate. Advance written permission must be obtained from you prior to initiation of individual evaluation procedures. Prior notice, both written and oral, requesting permission for testing will be given in English and the primary language of your home, unless it is clearly not feasible to do so. All individual evaluation procedures performed by the school system will be fair and nondiscriminatory.

The notice will inform you of the reasons the evaluations have been requested including other options considered and the reasons for rejecting these options, your right to information about each evaluation, the name and telephone number of the person to call if you have further questions, a statement of your right to refuse to consent to the evaluations with the understanding that a professional staff member may appeal your decision in order to obtain approval to conduct the evaluations, a statement of your right to be fully informed of the results of the evaluations and to have access to the records of your child, and a declaration that the requested procedures will not take place without your knowledge and written approval or until due process procedures have been exhausted. The notice will inform you to contact the school for notification of the times, dates, and places of the local screening and eligibility committees.

II. Eligibility

Notice of Eligibility

If your child is found eligible for special education services, you must be given notice, both written and oral, in English and the primary language of your home, unless it is clearly not feasible to do so, of the following: the reasons for the proposed action, including other options considered and the reasons for rejecting these options and the specifications of any tests or reports upon which such action is based; the names and positions of the persons determining the eligibility and recommending the level of service; a statement of the parental right to refuse the eligibility with the understanding that a professional staff member may appeal the parental refusal; a statement of the parental right to have access to the records of the student and to request an independent educational evaluation at public expense; a declaration that the level of service will be determined at the IEP conference with participation and approval by the parent; and a copy of Individualized Education Program Provisions and Procedural Safeguards and Due Process Provisions.

If your child is found ineligible for special education services, notice will include a statement of the specific and complete reasons for the denial, including the specification of any evaluation upon which such action is based; the names and positions of the persons who determined the denial; a statement of your right of access to the school records of your child; a statement of your right to request an independent educational evaluation at public expense for your child; and a statement of your right to appeal the denial of eligibility for special education services, and a copy of Procedural Safeguards and Due Process Provisions.

Permission for Placement

An individualized education program (IEP)/placement conference will take place when a change is proposed in the way in which educational services are provided to your child. You have the right to participate in the IEP conference and you will be notified orally and in writing of the conference. The notice will inform you of the purpose, time, date, and location of the IEP conference as well as who will be in attendance. An IEP will be developed prior to placement in a special education program, annually, and following a triennial reevaluation when eligibility for a special education program is reaffirmed. At the IEP conference, your permission will be required for assignment into, or change within, the special education program. If you refuse to give permission for the proposed placement, a professional staff member may appeal your decision in order to obtain approval to effect the placement. You may request a different placement by contacting the principal and requesting that the IEP/placement team reconvene. The IEP team has the responsibility to initiate requests for changes in program eligibility/placement.

IV. Appeals

Administrative Review

Area and central administrative review processes are voluntary and may be convened upon the agreement of both parent and professional staff members.

An administrative review committee will be established to mediate in those instances where an appeal request, in writing, is received by the area superintendent from the following: parents whose request for testing has been denied; professional staff following parent refusal to give permission for testing or placement; professional staff in those instances where an eligibility committee has been unable to determine whether a student is handicapped and in need of special education services; or parents regarding the eligibility/dismissal, placement of their child in high-incidence programs and/or the IEP. A central administrative review committee will be established to mediate these same issues in regard to low-incidence programs and nonpublic day school and residential placements. Low-incidence and nonpublic school appeals should be addressed, in writing, to the coordinator of due process.

Impartial Due Process Hearing

If an appeal has not been successfully mediated through the administrative review process or if parents or professional staff prefer to initiate an impartial due process hearing, the request should be made, in writing, to the coordinator of due process (low-incidence programs) or to the area superintendent (high-incidence programs) within six months of the time when the disagreement occurs on matters relating to identification, evaluation, or educational placement, or the provision of a free, appropriate public education.

You will be notified, in writing, following receipt of an appeal request of the time, date, and place the hearing will be convened; and of your right to be accompanied and advised by counsel and by individuals with special knowledge or training with respect to the problems of handicapped children; present evidence and confront, cross-examine, and compel the attendance of witnesses; prohibit the introduction of any evidence at the hearing that has not been disclosed at least five days before the hearing; obtain a written or electronic verbatim record of the hearing; obtain written findings of fact and decisions; have the child who is the subject of the hearing present; open the hearing to the public; and obtain information on free or low-cost legal and other relevant services. You also have the right to request an independent educational evaluation at public expense for your child and to obtain access to the school records of your child.

A decision made by the hearing office will be final unless a party to the hearing appeals to the Virginia Department of Education for an impartial review. A further option, that of bringing a civil action in the appropriate circuit court, is available following completion of all administrative procedures.

Placement During Appeals

If appeal procedures are initiated, your child will remain in the present educational placement until all due process procedures have been exhausted or until a proposed educational placement is accepted by both parties.

V. Other

Regulation 3401.1P includes documented procedures for the assignment of surrogate parents. Regulation 2701.1 provides documented procedures on access and confidentiality of records.

TRANSPORTATION

Introduction

Transportation helps us weave the fabrics of our lives together. Getting from here to there is critical in our mobile, late 20th century society. We are a society of travellers, not limited to the confines of our immediate neighborhoods for our economic and social lives.

At the same time, transit is more than getting from here to there. It encompasses a socialization process. When we travel, we see and interact with people who are diverse whether black, white, Hispanic, male, female, non-disabled or disabled.

Transportation is a unique, diverse subject. It is facilities, such as stations and overpasses; vehicles, including trains, subways, buses, and airplanes; and individuals who use those stations and vehicles as well as drive with licenses from their states.

Transportation is diffuse, with local conditions playing an overriding role. Older transit systems have much more difficult times achieving accessibility than newer systems, which can implement new technology and design concepts. It is easier to incorporate accessibility into new facilities and vehicles than to blend access into older vehicles and structures. Transportation issues give a new, more literal meaning to the Washington, D.C. axiom that where you stand on an issue depends on where you sit.

That kernel of truth was brought home to me in dramatic fashion during a trip with my children to New York City. Eschewing the automobile, we travelled completely by mass transportation. We left home on the public bus and took it to the subway, which we took to the AMTRAK. We took AMTRAK to New York City, where we continued on subways and buses until we reached our destination, the friendly confines of Grandpa's house in Brooklyn.

The route dramatically illustrated the different degrees and problems inherent in addressing travel problems of persons with disabilities.

In the Washington area a significant part of the bus fleet is already equipped with lifts. Additional accessible buses being ordered for conventional fixed route and the paratransit programs. Moreover, there are even some specially accessible taxicabs. Getting to the subway would not have been a major hassle for a person with disabilities.

When we got to the subway, since the system was a new one, there was an elevator at the station which, due to its prime location and the size of the subway station, was utilized more by non-disabled persons than persons with disabilities. It certainly helped us, loaded as we were with our packages. There were many signs to the station and lights flashed when the train was en route to the station. There were oral cues when the doors to the subway car were about to open and close. When we finally got on the subway we sat across from seats above which there was a sign indicating priority seating for senior citizens and persons with disabilities. The subway stop at which we disembarked was right at the AMTRAK terminal. Inside the AMTRAK station in order to change levels we took another elevator and proceeded to the train.

The AMTRAK train had limited accessibility, as would be expected from an older system which is in transition. There were signs in our car pointing toward the accessible bathroom on the train and indicating which exits were equipped with special assistive devices for persons in wheelchairs.

In New York City my children and I boarded the old subway, our luck of the draw landing us on of one of the older, less than spotless, cars. There were no persons with disabilities on the train. We had considered ourselves fortunate to be able to get to the correct subway without assistance. There were only stairs to the subway platform. The car had none of the necessary assistive devices for a person with a disability. When we got to our destination and were exiting the subway station we looked for an elevator but found only an escalator which had replaced the stairs. The bus that came was not equipped for persons in wheelchairs and a passerby told us that very few were. When we got off the bus we walked the remaining distance to our destination, noticing the carefully done, textured curb ramps.

In one day we had run the gamut. From the fully accessible system, to the transitional one, to the oldest one, the one which would be most difficult to make accessible.

Persons with different disabilities would have encountered diverse problems in the different systems we utilized that day. Having taken the route, it gave us an understanding of the various approaches that have been utilized in providing accessibility in transit as well as a sense of the magnitude of the problem that could catalyze the full range of tactics by advocates, from demonstrating at national transit meetings, to lobbying for the adoption of legislation, regulations, and policies, to litigating seeking redress against inaccessible systems.

There has been confrontation as well as cooperation. We are now in the age of implementation. This chapter gives an overview of diverse transportation-related requirements and concludes with a practical guide to assess the transportation needs and resources of employees, or others in a defined user community.

Driving

Nothing symbolizes mobility more in the 20th century than the automobile. We zoom around town, commute to work, drive our children's carpools, and head for the mall in millions of vehicles. For many of us there is no such thing as mass or public transportation. The car is the only way to travel.

For persons with disabilities driving entails problems with the vehicle as well as, far more significantly, the license to drive.

The vehicles can be addressed quickly, as there are no standards for accessible cars. It is not uncommon for persons with disabilities to design the special features they need to make their vehicles suitable for them. While this may result in an occasional Rube Goldbergesque vehicle, more commonly it entails hand controls for a person who cannot use his legs, special switching devices, or lifts for a wheelchair.

It is clear that hearing impaired persons do not require special features, though the mirrors in the vehicle do play a role of enhanced significance. Many deaf persons buy automobiles with AM-FM radios, not because they expect to listen to them, but for resale value.

Renting vehicles can be a problem. Much advance notice is required to obtain special parking permits or other identification to allow persons with disabilities to park in spaces specially designated for persons with disabilities. Some disabled persons bring their own portable hand controls with them and affix them to their rented vehicles.

Drivers' licenses pose more legal issues. States have to balance the needs of all their residents to travel and enjoy the roads safely. States, not the federal government, have control over drivers' licenses. Each state may regulate who is authorized to drive within it.

These licenses have one universally accepted, physical requirement: vision. In terms of the disability parlance of this book, vision may be said to be a bona fide qualification for which reasonable accommodation, i.e., corrective glasses or lenses, are allowed.

Disabling conditions commonly subject to more stringent regulation include epilepsy and seizure disorders, diabetes, cerebral palsy, muscular dystrophy, multiple sclerosis, heart condition, stroke, loss of limb, organic brain syndrome, and schizophrenia.

Disabling conditions are subject to periodic reviews and requirements indigenous to each state. Medical advisory boards are commonly involved on a periodic basis, which may or may not be specified. The requirements for licenses, including those requirements for persons with disabilities are subject to administrative hearings and judicial review under state law. At the end of this chapter is a chart of the Epilepsy Foundation of America enumerating the requirements related to epilepsy and drivers' licenses in each of the states. Other conditions are treated similarly.

The Americans with Disabilities Act (ADA) addresses the key transportation related issue of insurance, including automobile insurance. ADA makes clear that qualified individuals with disabilities cannot be denied insurance or subjected to different terms or conditions of insurance based on disability alone, if the disability does not pose increased risks. State insurance laws and regulations are not impacted by ADA's focus on actuarially based risks, classifications, and benefits.

Also related to the question of driving an automobile is the issue of parking the vehicle. As noted in Chapter 3, the United States Department of Transportation in 1991 was to issue guidelines to states for the establishment of a more uniform system of parking, drivers license plates, and placards for individuals with disabilities.

Federal Law And Regulatory Efforts: Rehabilitation Act and Mass Transit; · Americans with Disabilities Act

The two key nondiscrimination laws, section 504 of the Rehabilitation Act and the Americans with Disabilities Act, are closely related. The experiences in the implementation of the Rehabilitation Act set the stage for the provisions enacted into the ADA. Accordingly we begin with the Rehabilitation Act before exploring ADA, mindful that neither reaches passenger air travel. (Air travel, including the Air Carrier Access Act, is discussed later in this chapter.)

In the implementation of section 504 of the Rehabilitation Act no subject has generated such intense energy as that of accessible buses and mass transit. Demonstrations were a part of the scene before there were any regulations to implement section 504. Today, there are few such public clashes over section 504 — except when it comes to mass transit, especially buses.

The demonstrations, in local communities as well as at national transit industry meetings, have been about the design of the "accessible" bus as well as the level and nature of services that localities must provide. The subject has provoked litigation attacking the rules and their implementation by both disabled users of public mass transit as well as service providers.

The initial key legislation in this area was enacted in 1964, the Urban Mass Transportation Act. It declared that the elderly and persons with disabilities should have the same right to use mass transit and required "special efforts" in the planning and designing of mass transit programs toward that end. Subsequently, various transportation program acts, including the Surface Transportation Assistance Act and amendments thereto, have been adopted. These laws are administered by the United States Department of Transportation (DOT).

DOT, like the other federal agencies, has issued regulations to implement the application of section 504 of the Rehabilitation Act to recipients of federal financial assistance from the various agencies of the department.

The DOT 504 regulation contains the same basic prohibitions against employment discrimination that are elaborated upon at length in Chapter 2. The provisions mandate nondiscrimination against qualified individuals with physical or mental impairements and persons regarded as impaired in all phases of employment, even, as was established by a Supreme Court decision in *Conrail v. Darrone* 465 U.S. 24 (1984), if the purpose of the federal financial assistance is transit aid, not employment. These are generic provisions applicable to all DOT programs.

Similarly applicable across the board are the provisions relating to accessibility. New facilities are to be accessible as are alteration projects. In May, 1986, the technical standard for access with which construction by recipients must comply was changed to the Uniform Federal Accessibility Standard (UFAS) from ANSI A117.1-1961(r.1971).

The United States Department of Transportation regulation implementing section 504 as applied to mass transportation has been most controverted.

The initial DOT regulation required each mode of mass transportation to be accessible, within three years, though this was extendable up to 30 years where it entailed extraordinary expenses related to modifying facilities. This regulation was struck down by a federal appeals court as beyond the scope of section 504 since it required such significant expenditures. DOT could only mandate reasonable, modest, affirmative steps. This led the department to a second regulation on this subject under which recipients of aid certified that special efforts were made in their service area to provide transportation that persons with disabilities could use.

On May 23, 1986, the Department of Transportation issued a new regulation applying the nondiscrimination mandate under section 504 to the Surface Transportation Assistance Act. Amendments to the latter required the Department of Transportation to issue regulations establishing the minimum criteria for the provision of transportation services to elderly persons and persons with disabilities. The rules were to provide a process to monitor compliance as well as public participation so that affected and concerned individuals and organizations have notice and the opportunity to comment on the DOT recipients' activities.

This Department of Transportation regulation required recipients of aid to prepare a program for providing transportation services to persons with disabilities, utilizing a public participation process which includes consulting with persons with disabilities. The program was to be submitted to the Department of Transportation by May 23, 1987.

Recipients may meet their obligations under the rule by providing either special services, such as dial-a-van, taxi voucher, an accessible bus system (either a scheduled or on-call accessible bus system) or a mixed system (one having both special service and accessible bus elements). The recipient must meet the following service criteria:

1. All persons who, by reason of handicap, are physically unable to use the recipient's bus service for the general public must be eligible to use the service for persons with disabilities.
2. Service must be provided to a person with a disability within 24 hours of a request of it.
3. Restrictions or priorities based on trip purpose are not allowed.
4. Fares must be comparable to fares charged the general public for the same or similar trip.

5. The service for persons with disabilities must operate throughout the same days and hours as the service for the general public.
6. The service for persons with disabilities must be available throughout the same service area as the service for the general public.

As issued, the DOT regulation limited a federal recipient's obligation to 3 percent of the recipient's average operating costs over the current and two previous fiscal years. The cost cap was challenged sucessfully, leading to a major policy shift by DOT. In October, 1990 following a federal appeals court decision that the 3 percent cost cap was arbitrary and capricious, *ADAPT v. Skinner*, 881 F. 2d 1184 (3rd. Cir.1989), the Department of Transportation revised its section 504 regulation to eliminate the cost cap. The Department also made clear that it will require any grantee which changes the mode of accessible service delivery from special service to accessible bus to continue to provide special service at least at the level it now provides. This "maintenance of effort" provision was to facilitate compliance with other regulations the Department will be issuing under the ADA. While revising its section 504 regulation, DOT also made clear its policies were that all new buses were to be accessible and that supplemental paratransit services (subject to the limitation of undue financial burden) were required for individuals who could not use fixed route transit. Recipients of federal aid from the Department of Transportation must also comply with the ADA.

Subways

The issue of accessible mass transit in urban areas has perennially been one of conflict over the accessibility of subway systems. Consumers with disabilities assert their right to full access and full participation. On the other hand, operators of the systems, recipients of federal aid, raise vociferous objections as to the cost of accessibility, especially where older facilities are concerned.

It is accepted that accessibility is required in new subway facilities as well as in alterations to existing facilities. This has always been the rule under the Rehabilitation Act, as well as under the Architectural Barriers Act. The 1986 DOT regulation implementing section 504 requires compliance with the Uniform Federal Accessibility Standard, superseding ANSI A117.1-1961(r.1971) as the technical document. While seemingly a very straightforward proposition, these rules have occasioned litigation, as for example when the new Washington, D.C., subway system was set to open. All was in place except the elevators for persons with disabilities. The United States District Court for the District of Columbia enjoined the use of inaccessible stations and rejected pleas of the local transit agency, the Washington Metropolitan Transportation Authority, to operate the stations while the elevators were being finished. When the Chicago Transit Authority renovated several stations in the downtown area, elevators had to be installed. At Union Station in Washington, D.C., the Departments of Interior and Transportation removed the elevator from the upper to the lower tracks when renovating the facility. They were ordered to reinstall the elevator, which provides services to passengers, disabled or non-disabled.

The 1986 Department of Transportation amendment to the section 504 regulation means that metropolitan areas having both subway and bus systems can meet their nondiscrimination obligations by complying with the requirements for bus service elaborated upon at length earlier in this chapter. This is seemingly based on the proposition that, viewing the system as a whole, the bus and subway components are alternative, interchangeable, complementary components of the system.

In discussing subway systems, it is important to note that with respect to the New York City system, litigation against inaccessible subways under state law led to a finding that the structures were out of compliance, a result which in turn catalyzed the passage of state law ensuring persons with disabilities rights of access and rights of participation in the transit management process.

Commuter Rail

There are presently no nondiscrimination regulations under the Rehabilitation Act affecting commuter rail transit. There are standards of access for the vehicles and the stations. Simultaneously with issuing the final regulation affecting mass transit, DOT invited comments on issues affecting commuter rail and persons with disabilities.

The proposal issued by the Department of Transportation concerning commuter rail invited comments on the criteria for commuter rail service, including whether there should be full main line accessibility, or a more limited, key station access. DOT also solicited comments on questions, including response time, fares, and times of service, related to alternative service for those persons with disabilities unable to utilize the commuter rail system. This rulemaking was initiated in conjunction with the issuance of the rule related to mass transportation. DOT recognizes that commuter stations are not integrally linked or part of regular bus systems and thus cannot be viewed, as the subway stations were, as related components in a single system. DOT proposed keeping in effect the technical standards relating to the accessibility of vehicles and facilities, though UFAS is now to be the standard for facilities.

The rules proposed by DOT were never finalized, having gotten caught up in the litigation related to the cost limitation as well as the movement toward enactment and implementation of the Americans with Disabilities Act (ADA). When DOT, pursuant to the ADA, issues rules, due by July 26, 1991, for commuter rail entities, DOT also will issue substantively substantially identical rules for commuter rail programs subject to section 504 of the Rehabilitation Act.

Rail

The Department of Transportation requires that new rail stations, as well as alteration projects, be accessible to persons with disabilities. As was the case with subway facilities, the technical standard is now UFAS, superseding ANSI. The Department also prescribes certain additional features related to service and facilities that must be provided. These include teletypewriters for the deaf, boarding areas, ticketing, station flow and circulation. By 1984 recipients of federal aid were required to have made accessible at least the station in each Standard Metropolitan Statistical Area (SMSA) that had the greatest annual passenger volume. Stations within 50 miles of a SMSA were under a similar direction to be accessible by 1984. By 1989 all stations in an SMSA were to be accessible. The approach with rail vehicles was also along the lines of the five year mandate. Within five years each passenger train had to have at least one coach car accessible, one sleeping car, if provided, and food service available, either in an accessible food service car or at the seat of the person with disabilities. Assistance is to be provided to meet the needs of handicapped travellers.

It should be observed that under state laws many rail facilities would be considered places of public accommodation and subject to the mandate of nondiscrimination. This means that under state laws new activities as well as renovations and alterations have to be accessible. State laws generally do not mandate retrofitting buildings that met the building code when constructed. See Appendix I for a directory of state laws prohibiting discrimination in places of public accommodation.

Americans with Disability Act (ADA)

The Rehabilitation Act and the heatedly debated and litigated rules under it were the forerunner of the Americans with Disabilities Act. ADA in very specific statutory provisions in Title II (nondiscrimination by state and local government entities) and Title III (nondiscrimination in public accommodations) builds on the concept of program accessibility in transit—vehicles, facilities, and services—that evolved under section 504 of the Rehabilitation Act.

The Rehabilitation Act as predicate for the Americans with Disabilities Act is clearly illustrated in Title II of the ADA. For example, under the ADA new bus and rail vehicles that are purchased or leased after August 25, 1990 must be accessible. If used vehicles are procured after that date, there must be a good faith effort to purchase accessible, usable vehicles. There is a similar provision with respect to remanufactured vehicles having usable life of five (5) years or more. If a public entity has a fixed route public transit system, then the entity must also serve the disabled individuals who cannot use that system by providing paratransit or special services. The level of service must be comparable to the fixed route service, subject only to the limitation that providing such service is not an undue hardship on the entity.

Entities operating demand response bus systems must also procure accessible new vehicles after August 25, 1990, unless the system provides an equivalent level of services to persons with and without disabilities.

All new transit facilities and alterations of existing facilities must be accessible. Moreover, if an alteration is to a primary function of a facility is undertaken, then an accessible path of travel to the altered area and the bathrooms, telephones, and drinking fountains serving that area must be accessible and usable to the extent that the added accessibility costs are not disproportionate to the overall cost of the alterations. The law requires all existing intercity stations (sic. AMTRAK) to be accessible as soon as practicable and no later than 20 years after enactment, July 26, 2010.

Also under Title II, public rail systems must have one accessible car per train by July 26, 1995 . Existing "key" stations (a concept from the Rehab Act indicating high ridership, transfer, or feeder stations) in rapid rail, commuter rail and light rail, must be accessible by July 26, 1993, three years after enactment of ADA (through significant extensions for 20 years are possible, even to 30 years for certain rapid and light rail entities).

Regulations are to be issued by July 26, 1991, by the DOT to implement the Title II transit requirements of ADA. The rule related to facilities and vehicles must meet the Minimum Guidelines and Requirements for Accessible Design (MGRAD) to be issued by the U.S. Architectural and Transportation Barriers Compliance Board that are due out by April 26, 1991. It is expected that the Uniform Federal Accessibility Standard (UFAS) will be the point of departure for the new MGRADs. Congressional reports in connection with ADA indicate a figure of 30 percent as an acceptable proportion for additional alteration costs, though the precise proportion will be established in the regulation. DOT began to meet its rulemaking responsibilities in October, 1990, issuing final rules on accessible vehicles and rail cars, while also inviting comment on those rules.

Violations of this part of Title II of ADA can be redressed through private rights of action in court in which specific relief and attorneys' fees are recoupable or through complaints to the United States Department of Transportation.

Under Title III of ADA the focus is on transportation provided by private entities as public accommodations. (See Chapter 3 for a discussion of those requirements including those related to accessibility, barrier removal obligations, reasonable modifications to policies, and providing auxiliary services.) Title III's transit provisions may be approached by distinguishing between public transportation services provided by private entities not primarily engaged in the business of transporting people and those which are so primarily engaged.

For those entities not primarily engaged in providing transit services (such as a hotel/motel, private school, or other private business which operate shuttle services between locations) all new fixed route vehicles ordered after August 25, 1990, and carrying more than 16 passengers must be accessible. If a smaller vehicle is used (16 or less passengers) on a fixed route service system, then the vehicle need not be accessible if the system, when viewed in its entirety, provides equivalent services for disabled and nondisabled persons.

If a private entity not primarily in the transit business is operating a demand response system, rather than a fixed route system, the rules are the same but the vehicle with capacity for more than 16 passengers need not be accessible, if the system, when viewed in its entirety, provides equivalent services to disabled and nondisabled persons.

An entity, not primarily engaged in the transit business, which has over-the-road buses is not required to modify the current stock of such vehicles to be accessible. But when purchasing or leasing new vehicles the entity must comply with regulations, due out by July 26, 1991, from the United States Department of Transportation.

With respect to entities primarily engaged in the provision of public transportation services, Title III provides that the after August 25, 1990, all vehicles (other than an automobile or van with a capacity of less than 8 persons) that are purchased or leased must be accessible and usable by persons with disabilities. If such vehicles are to be used exclusively in a demand response system, which system when viewed in its entirety provides an equivalent level of service for persons with and without disabilities, then the vehicle need not be accessible. If a new van with a seating capacity of less than 8 persons is purchased/leased after August 25, 1990, such vehicle must be accessible unless the entity can demonstrate that the system for which the van is being purchased/leased, when viewed in its entirety, provides equivalent services to disabled and nondisabled persons.

Throughout the legislative process there was intense debate concerning the over-the-road bus services by private transit companies. The debate culminated in mandating that the Office of Technology Assessment ("OTA") complete a study by July 26, 1993, on the needs of disabled persons for access to over-the-road buses and services and the cost-effective methods of meeting those needs. OTA is a research arm of the Congress. The study is to be submitted to the President and the Congress. Based on the study and within one year after it is submitted, i.e., by July 26, 1994, the Secretary of Transportation will issue regulations requiring accessibility in such vehicles. Smaller providers, as must be defined in the DOT regulation, will have seven years to comply, one year longer than the larger providers. The President has discretion, based on the OTA study, to extend the deadlines by one year. Interim regulations on over-the-road buses are due from DOT by July 26, 1991, a year after ADA was enacted. The interim DOT regulation shall not require the purchase of boarding assistive devices. The final DOT rules may not require accessible bathrooms on over-the-road buses if the installation of such bathrooms would result in a loss of seating capacity.

With respect to private entities primarily in the transit business, all rail cars purchased/leased after August 25, 1990, must be accessible. Remanufactured cars with a useful life of ten (10) years or more, to the maximum extent feasible, must be accessible and usable. Historic rail cars (30 years old or more and the manufacturer no longer in that business) can be exempt if compliance with the access requirements would alter the historic character of the car our would result in a violation of the Federal Railroad Safety Act.

As noted in Chapter 3, the Attorney General has the responsibility to issue regulations related to public accommodations. DOT must issue transit related regulations. Both Title III regulations are due out by July 26, 1991, one year after enactment. In October 1990, the DOT began to meet its responsibilities by issuing final rules under ADA with regard to the purchase of vehicles by private entities, requesting comments on the rules as well. The final rule here too, as for public entities under Title II, must meet MGRADs that the U.S. Architectural Transportation Barriers Compliance Board must issue by April 26, 1991. Violations of Title III, as noted in chapter 3, are redressable in court by individuals who may obtain specific relief and attorney's fees, as well as by complaints to the Department of Transportation and Attorney General, as appropriate. The Attorney General may recover damages.

Air Travel

Travel by air presents numerous issues. These include airport accessibility as well as air carrier discrimination and air safety rules.

The issue of facilities is straightforward. Both new structures as well as renovations or alterations to existing buildings must be accessible. In much the same manner as rail stations, the standard is, as of 1986, UFAS, superseding ANSI. Passenger and baggage loading, parking, and waiting areas are all to be made accessible, even if not explicitly required in the technical standard. Teletypewriters also are to be provided. Deaf and blind persons are to be given timely information and guide dogs are allowed. Assistance in boarding is to be given mobility impaired persons. It is required without advance notice unless major assistance is required. Under the Rehab Act, terminal operators had until 1984 to achieve basic program accessibility in their facilities. These provisions were not the center of the controversy.

The controverted issues related to passenger use of air carriers. The Civil Aeronautics Board issued its nondiscrimination regulation, setting forth a series of requirements for carriers. The rules were challenged by the Paralyzed Veterans of America and other organizations representing persons with disabilities when they were applied only to small commercial carriers that receive direct federal subsidies. In June 1986, the United States Supreme Court in *Department of Transportation v. Paralyzed Veterans of America* 477 U.S. 597 (1986), reversing the lower court, upheld the government's contention that the regulation only applied to small carriers. The Court ruled that section 504 applied only to those entities which are, in fact, recipients of federal aid, not to those persons, such as the passengers with disabilities, who benefitted from the assistance. The recipients of aid who were subject to the mandate of the Rehabilitation Act were the airport operators and not, as a general rule, the airlines. Those small airlines which did receive subsidies from the government were also recipients and were also covered. While major carriers who used the airports and the air traffic controllers benefit from the assistance, the carriers were not recipients of federal aid and thus not subject to section 504. The program or activity funded was one of the operators, not those who rode or used the facility.

Congress reacted swiftly to the decision, enacting the Air Carrier Access Act of 1986, P.L.99-435, amending the Federal Aviation Act to prohibit discrimination by air carriers against qualified persons with physical or mental impairments or persons regarded as impaired. Like the ADA, and unlike the Rehabilitation Act, the application of this law is not linked to the airline receiving federal financial assistance. After enactment of the Air Carrier Access Act, the focus of the debate over air carrier policies shifted back to the Department of Transportation from Congress.

While the Air Carrier Access Act required the Department of Transportation to issue regulations within 120 days after its 1986 enactment, the rules delineating the rights and responsibilities of airline industry and persons with disabilities were not finalized until the spring of 1990. The rules prohibit airlines from limiting the number of disabled persons on a flight but do allow airlines to require a particular individual (not necessarily all disabled persons) to have an attendant, e.g., when the individual has a severe mental impairment. Airlines may not establish special advance notice requirements for disabled persons, but may require advance notice for special equipment, such as a respirator. Airlines can refuse service to disabled passenger if it would be inimicable to the safety of the flight and a written explanation is provided within ten days of the flight. Seating restrictions are prohibited except to comply with a Federal Aviation Administration safety rule. Boarding assistance and baggage accommodations for manual and electric wheelchairs are also required.

The rules require accessibility in new airport facilities and alteration projects. Access applies inside airplanes too, such a moveable aisle armrests in new or refurnished airplanes. New wide-body airplanes (767 and 747 aircraft) are to have accessible bathrooms and, by April 5, 1992, on-board wheelchairs for movement inside the airplane.

The Air Carrier Access Act is enforceable by complaints to the United States Department of Transportation as well as through private rights of action filed in federal courts, in which specific relief, damages, and attorney's fees, have been awarded.

In passing it must be noted that the state and local laws are of limited application. The laws against discrimination in places of public accommodation do apply to airports (See Appendix I). However, the state laws do not address interstate air carriers.

Highways

The Department of Transportation regulation under section 504 also requires accessibility when new rest areas are constructed, as well as when federal aid is used to improve the rest area, or when the roadway adjacent to or in the vicinity is being reconstructed or otherwise altered. Under the regulation, rest areas, curb cuts, pedestrian overpasses, underpasses, and ramps must be accessible. Recipients had until 1984 to achieve program accessibility in their existing facilities.

The technical standard for accessibility was ANSI A117.1-1961 (r.1971). However, slopes of up to 1:10 (10%) were allowed, in contrast to the 1:12 (8.33%) grade in ANSI, unless alternate safe means of crossing were provided for mobility impaired persons or it was otherwise unfeasible. The 1986 amendment to the department regulation made the UFAS the technical standard, superseding ANSI. However, here again the maximum slope ratios remained at 1:10, not the standard 1:12.

Transportation Planning: A Tool For A Defined Community

The issue of transportation cannot be viewed in isolation. To do so would be to disregard the assimilative, melding role of transportation as a means to connect the disparate facets of our lives. This is classically observed in defined communities such as a university or work situation.

Here is a form that may be utilized to ascertain needs of persons with disabilities such as employees, visitors, students, or others whose presence is anticipated in a particular defined setting. This form can be modified to fit the user's particular needs. NOTE: This information should NOT be the predicate for a decision to employ, admit, or otherwise allow the participation of a particular person with disabilities. After that decision has been made it would be appropriate to make these inquiries:

Needs Form*

Please complete the enclosed form. It will enable us to most efficiently ascertain the needs of our community and work with local officials to attain transportation services for you. Please indicate which services you utilize in a typical week. Do not hesitate to indicate the use of more than one method of transportation but do indicate the frequency of different modes. If a question does not apply to you, indicate so by noting "NA."

Company Name: _____

Facility Location: _____

Optional: Name & Telephone No. _____

Disabling Condition(s) _____

1. Do you presently travel independently, i.e., without assistance of another person? If no, under "Remarks" please indicate the nature of the assistance you receive including any costs related thereto.
2. Indicate which method(s) you presently use most frequently to get to the site: drive alone, carpool, regular bus, paratransit, cab, train?
3. Are there curb cuts or curb ramps along the route to the mode of transportation identified in Question 2, or are there conventional curbs? In the space below under "Remarks" identify where there is a need for curb cuts or curb ramps.
4. When you arrive by the mode of transportation you identified in Question 2, are there curb cuts or curb ramps along the route, or are there conventional curbs? In the space below under "Remarks" identify where there is a need for curb cuts or curb ramps.

*Reprinted with permission from the **Handicapped Requirements Handbook**, Thompson Publishing Company, Washington, D.C.

5. If you drive, please state whether you require a special wider, nearer parking place for a person with disabilities. If so, please indicate the nature of your disability. Preference in allocating the wider, nearer spaces will be given to those who are non-ambulatory or mobility impaired, as well as to those such persons who are unable to drive but who carpool with drivers. Other persons with disabilities, persons who are blind or have low vision, and persons with hearing impairments will also be given designated spaces.

6. Does the vehicle used most frequently have a sticker and/or license plates authorizing parking in specially designated spaces?

7. If you take the bus, is it door-to-door regular service or does it have to be specially ordered? If specially ordered, please note under "Remarks" the time in advance that you must order and any other limitations.

8. If you take specialized door-to-door service, is there a regular fixed route transit on an accessible (lift-equipped) vehicle available?

9. Do you have the ability to get to fixed route service?

10. Are there lift-equipped buses on the service line nearest you? What is their frequency in morning and evening?

11. If you take the train, are there usually accessible cars?

12. How long does it take you to get to/from the site by the mode you use most regularly?

13. a. How much does it cost you to get to/from the site?
    b. Are there subsidies for transit available to you?

14. Have you ever had to leave early or been unable to stay or attend a function because of a transportation related problem?

15. Have you ever been refused service because of your disability? If so, please explain under "Remarks."

16. Do you have a valid state driver's license for a car? van? truck? Any restrictions or history of suspensions or revocation? If so, add under "Remarks."

17. If you have occasion to leave the site periodically during the day, indicate the frequency of departures on a monthly/weekly basis, noting which, and indicate the form of transit used, (i.e., auto, carpool, cab, regular bus, paratransit, train).

18. What method of transportation did you utilize before you used the method identified in response to question 2: auto, carpool, cab, regular bus, paratransit, train?

19. On what basis did you determine to utilize the method you use most frequently to get here? Cost? Schedules? Accessibility? Personal convenience?

20. How did you learn about the availability of accessible transportation in this area? Friend? Radio/TV? Called Transportation Agency? Office told you?

Remarks: Item #___ _____

Item #___ _____

A Final Note

Transportation is the connecting link for the different generations, for people with and without disabilities. Transportation links the diverse facets of our lives: jobs, housing, schools, shopping, recreation; making each of them, and in turn, each of us, whether or not we have a disability, more accessible. It is more than getting from here to there.

"Driving & Epilepsy" Chart

The chart on the following pages is reprinted with permission from the National Spokesperson, Epilepsy Foundation of America, March 1990. The only change subsequent to that publication has been incorporated here. Information contained in this chart is current as of March 1991. This chart was developed for information purposes and is not a substitute for legal advice. Consult with your state Department of Motor Vehicles or the Epilepsy Foundation of America for additional information.

Driving & Epilepsy

State	Seizure-Free Period	Periodic Medical Updates Required After Licensing	Doctors Required To Report Seizures	DMV* Appeal of License Denial
Alabama	1 year	Annually for 10 years from date of last seizure	No	Yes
Alaska	6 months	No, but Department of Motor Vehicles may require annual physical exam	No	Yes 15 days
Arizona	1 year, with exceptions	At discretion of Motor Vehicle Division	No	Yes 15 days
Arkansas	1 year	At discretion of Department of Motor Vehicles	No	Yes 20 days
California	None	as above	Yes	Yes 10 days
Colorado	None	as above	No	Yes
Connecticut	3 months	Every 6 months	No	Yes

State	Seizure-Free Period	Periodic Medical Updates Required After Licensing	Doctors Required To Report Seizures	DMV* Appeal of License Denial
Delaware	None	Annually	Yes	Yes
District of Columbia	1 year	Annually until 5 years seizure-free	No	Yes Within 5 days if suspended or revoked
Florida	1 year	At discretion of Medical Advisory Board	No	Yes
Georgia	1 year. Less if only nocturnal seizures	At discretion of Department of Motor Vehicles	No	Within 15 days
Hawaii	1 year	as above	No	Yes
Idaho	1 year. Less with doctor recommendation medication change	Every 6 months or annually	No	Yes
Illinois	None	At discretion of Medical Advisory Board	No	Yes
Indiana	None	as above	No	Yes
Iowa	6 months. Less if seizures nocturnal	Every 2 years	No	Yes

State	Seizure-Free Period	Periodic Medical Updates Required After Licensing	Doctors Required To Report Seizures	DMV* Appeal of License Denial
Kansas	1 year	Annually, until 5 years seizure-free	No	Yes Within 30 days
Kentucky	3 months	At discretion of Medical Advisory Board	No	Within 20 days
Louisiana	1 year, with exceptions	as above	No	No
Maine	1 year or 6 months	as above	No	Yes
Maryland	3 months	as above	No	Within 15 days
Massachusetts	6 months	At discretion of Medical Advisory Board	No	Within 14 days
Michigan	6 months. Less with doctor recommendation	as above	No	Within 14 days
Minnesota	Generally, 6 months	as above	No	Yes
Mississippi	1 year	as above	No	Yes
Missouri	None	At license renewal	No	No
Montana	6 months	No	No	Yes
Nebraska	1 year	No	No	Yes

State	Seizure-Free Period	Periodic Medical Updates Required After Licensing	Doctors Required To Report Seizures	DMV* Appeal of License Denial
Nevada	3 months	Annually	Yes	Yes
New Hampshire	1 year	No	No	Within 30 days
New Jersey	1 year. Less on recommendation of Neurological Disorder Committee	Every 6 months for 2 years, thereafter annually	Yes	Within 10 days
New Mexico	1 year	At discretion of Medical Advisory Board	No	Within 20 days
New York	1 year. Less with doctor recommendation.	At discretion of Department of Motor Vehicles	No	Within 30 days
North Carolina	None	Annually, or less at discretion of Department of Motor Vehicles	No	Within 10 days
North Dakota	1 year. Restricted licenses available after six months	Annually for at least 5 years	No	Within 10 days
Ohio	None	Every 6 months or 1 year until seizure-free 5 years	No	Within 30 days

State	Seizure-Free Period	Periodic Medical Updates Required After Licensing	Doctors Required To Report Seizures	DMV* Appeal of License Denial
Oklahoma	1 year, with exceptions	At discretion of Department of Public Safety	No	Yes
Oregon	6 months, with exceptions	Every 6 or 12 months until 2 years seizure-free	Yes	Within 20 days
Pennsylvania	1 year. Less if nocturnal or prolonged auras	At discretion of Medical Advisory Board	Yes	No
Puerto Rico	None	as above	No	Within 20 days
Rhode Island	Usually 18 months. Less at discretion of Department of Transportation	as above	No	Yes
South Carolina	6 months	Every 6 months	No	Within 10 days
South Dakota	12 months. Less with doctor recommendation	Every 6 months until 12 months seizure-free	No	No
Tennessee	No set seizure-free period	At discretion of Medical Advisory Board	No	Within 20 days

State	Seizure-Free Period	Periodic Medical Updates Required After Licensing	Doctors Required To Report Seizures	DMV* Appeal of License Denial
Texas	1 year. Less if nocturnal or due to medication change	At discretion of Medical Advisory Board	No	No
Utah	3 months	Annually until seizure-free 5 years	No	Within 10 days
Vermont	24 months, or 6 months with doctor recommendation	Every 6 months until 24 months seizure-free	No	Yes
Virginia	1 year or 6 months	At discretion of Medical Advisory Board	No	No
Washington	6 months	as above	No	Yes
West Virginia	1 year	as above	No	10 days
Wisconsin	3 months	Every 6 months for 2 years. Annually thereafter until seizure-free 5 years	No	Yes

State	Seizure-Free Period	Periodic Medical Updates Required After Licensing	Doctors Required To Report Seizures	DMV* Appeal of License Denial
Wyoming	1 year, with exceptions	Annually until seizure-free 2 years, thereafter upon license renewal	No	Yes

Epilepsy
FOUNDATION OF AMERICA
4351 Garden City Drive • Landover, MD 20785

* Time frames within which one must request an administrative hearing are given when known. Every state allows for appeal of license denial through the courts.

** Note: Non-driver I.D. cards are available in every state.

Summing Up

The apocryphal story is told of the person who flew across the country with his pet dog in storage in the cargo hold of the airplane. Unfortunately when the plane landed, our traveller was saddened by the news that his dog had died during the flight. When he sought help from the airline and showed them what the claim check said about their liability, the airline told him he was out of luck because the dog had "defective fur."

For many years persons with physical or mental disabilities have been excluded, pitied, or otherwise treated as less than integral, equal members of society, in essence treated as having "defective fur."

The laws and solutions discussed in this book have been an effort to make all people understand that there really is no such thing as defective fur.

WORDS, AND PARTS THEREOF, FOR THE WISE

In every area of our lives various words and special terms related to the field are used. The "jargon" or "buzz words" of a subject are often a shorthand for participants, a dialect utilized by persons intimately involved.

Here are some key terms which have appeared in this book, as well as others of value.

AB	Able-bodied.
ABA	Architectural Barriers Act of 1968.
Accessible	Approachable, functional and usable by persons with disabilities, independently, safely, and with dignity.
Accommodation	A change, as in a program or a job, to make it accessible.
ADA	Americans with Disabilities Act.
Adaptable	Capable of being made accessible at a later date. Often used to refer to housing.
AIDS	Acquired Immune Deficiency Syndrome.
ANSI	American National Standard Institute which issues building standards, including A117.1 affecting accessibility.

Architectural Barrier	A physical barrier which prohibits or limits the use of a building or facility.
Architectural Barriers Act of 1968	ABA. Federal law requiring federal and federally assisted buildings and facilities to be accessible to, and usable by, persons with disabilities.
ATBCB	Architectural and Transportation Barriers Compliance Board, the federal agency responsible for enforcing the ABA. Federal locus of technical work related to accessibility.
Auxiliary Aids and Services	Used in ADA to include such services and actions as providing qualified interpreters or other effective methods of making aurally delivered materials available to individuals with hearing impairments; qualified readers, taped texts or other effective methods of making visually delivered materials available to individuals with visual impairments; or the acquisition or modification of equipment or devices.
Barrier Free	Usually used with the word environment. It connotes the total absence of obstacles; 100 percent accessible.
Braille	A system of writing for persons who are blind or vision impaired that uses raised dots aligned to be characters and letters.
Bureaucrat	Collector of papers. Master of none.
Catheterization	Use of a tube to remove a fluid from the system, commonly urine from certain persons with disabilities.

Continuum of Services	The range of educational and related services to be available to persons eligible under the Education for All Handicapped Children Act (now IDEA).
CP	Cerebral Palsy.
CRRA	Civil Rights Restoration Act of 1988.
DD	Developmentally Disabled. Often used to refer to persons who are under 18 and who have conditions which are expected to continue indefinitely and which condition is attributable to mental retardation, cerebral palsy, autism, epilepsy.
Demand Responsive System	A system of providing designated public transit on other than a fixed route system.
Developmental Disability	A severe, chronic disability of a person which: (a) is attributable to a mental or physical impairment or combination of mental or physical impairments; (b) is manifested before the person attains the age of twenty-two; (c) is likely to continue indefinitely; (d) results in substantial functional limitations in three or more of the following areas of major life activity: (1) self care, (2) receptive and expressive language, (3) learning, (4) mobility, (5) self-direction, (6) capacity for independent living, and (7) economic sufficiency; and (e) reflects the person's need for a combination and sequence of special, interdisciplinary, or generic care, treatment or other services which are lifelong or extended duration and are individually planned and coordinated.

DHEW
(HEW)

United States Department of Health, Education, & Welfare, now reorganized into the Department of Education (DOE or ED) and the Department of Health and Human Services (DHHS or HHS).

Disabled Individual
(Disabled Person)
(Handicapped Person)

See Person with a Disability.

Discrimination

Differential treatment or practices either intentionally or effectively by action/policy/practice.

DOE (or ED)

United States Department of Education.

DOJ

United States Department of Justice.

DOT

United States Department of Transportation.

Down Syndrome

A form of mental retardation, now believed to be traceable to chromosomal abnormality.

Due Process

A hearing in which both sides have the opportunity to present witnesses and evidence on their behalf, and to cross-examine the witnesses of the other as well as contest the introduction of evidence by the other side, all which occurs under the direction of a neutral third party—the judge or hearing examiner.

Dyslexia

An example of a learning disability which limits the ability of the person to read.

EAHCA

Education For All Handicapped Children Act, P.L. 94-142. Federal law, renamed in 1990, Individuals with Disabilities Education Act, P.L. 101-476.

Emotionally Disabled	Person with a mental illness or receiving psychological or psychiatric treatment.
Epilepsy	Neurological disorder of the brain which may manifest itself in "blanking out", petit mal; convulsive thrashing, grand mal seizures; or other ways.
Fair Housing Amendments	1988 revisions to the Federal Fair Housing Law prohibiting discrimination against persons with disabilities.
Free Appropriate Public Education (FAPE)	The educational and related services to which a person is entitled under EAHCA (now IDEA).
Federal Financial Assistance	Any grant, loan, contract (other than procurement contract or contract of insurance or guaranty) or any other aid provided by a federal agency in the form of either funds, services, or interest in real or personal property.
Fixed Route System	A system of providing designated public transportation on a vehicle along a prescribed route according to a fixed system. This is the conventional transit route system.
Handicap	A physical or mental limitation, or a condition regarded as such an impairment.
Handicapper	Person with a disability. Example of a local term. Used only in Michigan.
HHS	United States Department of Health and Human Services.
HUD	United States Department of Housing and Urban Development.

IDEA	Individuals with Disabilities Education Act, P.L. 101-476.
Independent Living Center (ILC)	Local community center at which services, training, and information are available to persons with disabilities.
Individual Education Program (IEP)	The written program of instruction, education and related services, developed under EAHCA (now IDEA), usually on an annual basis.
Interpreter	Individual who translates for another, here for persons who are hearing impaired or deaf.
Learning Disability	A disorder in one or more of the basic psychological processes involved in understanding or in using language, spoken or written, which may manifest itself in an imperfect ability to think, read, write, spell or do mathematical calculations.
Least Restrictive Environment (LRE)	The placement of a child entitled to services under EAHCA (now IDEA). The LRE is where the child receives educational and related services.
Mainstreaming	The educational concept of placing students who are disabled and non-disabled together, to the extent appropriate for the particular individual. The term also is equated with the term "integration."
Major Life Activities	This means functions such as caring for one's self, performing manual tasks, walking, seeing, hearing, speaking, breathing, learning, and working.
MD	Muscular Dystrophy.

Mental Retardation (MR)	A significant subaverage general intelligence level determined in accordance with standard measurements, existing concurrently with impairment in adaptive behavior. Note, there are levels of retardation.
MGRAD	Minimum Guidelines and Requirements for Accessible Design, issued by the ATBCB, are the basis of federal accessibility requirements.
Multihandicapped	More than one impairment simultaneously.
MS	Multiple Sclerosis.
OCR	Office for Civil Rights. Historically referred to the agency of DHEW. Now usually refers to an agency in ED.
Paraplegia (Para)	The condition of two limbs, usually the legs, being paralyzed.
Paratransit	Transportation for persons who are disabled (or elderly) that is alternative to regular fixed route transportation services. It includes transit such as provided by demand-responsive, call-in, and door-to-door, systems.
Person with a Disability	Individual with a physical or mental impairment which substantially limits a major life activity, who has a record of such impairment or individual who is regarded as having such an impairment.

Physical or Mental Impairment

Any physiological disorder or condition, cosmetic disfigurement, or anatomical loss affecting one or more of the following body systems: neurological musculoskeletal, special sense organs; respiratory, including speech organs; cardiovascular; reproductive; digestive; genito-urinary; hemic and lymphatic; skin; and endocrine. Also includes any mental or psychological disorder, such as mental retardation, organic brain syndrome, emotional or mental illness, and specific learning disabilities.

Physically Challenged

Person with physical disabilities. Newest term coming into use.

Post-Polio

The condition of having had polio.

Program Accessibility

The concept of making accessible all services or benefits to qualified persons with disabilities.

Public Accommodation

Include, but are not limited to, places open to the public, places serving food or drink such as restaurants and bars; places of lodging such as hotels, motels; convention centers, lecture halls, concert halls, movies, stadia and other public gathering, exhibition or entertainment places; retail stores and shopping centers; service establishments such as offices of a health care provider, hospital, lawyer, accountant, insurance, travel, bank, barber, shoe repair services, cleaners, gas stations; transit facilities; places of exercise or recreation such as gyms, spas, zoos, amusement parks or parks; places of public display or collection such as libraries and museums; schools; and social service centers such as day care, senior citizen centers and homeless shelters. Generally excludes facilities of religious institutions and private clubs not covered by the Civil Rights Act of 1964.

PWA　　Person with AIDS.

Quadriplegia (Quad)　　The condition of all four limbs, both arms and legs, being paralyzed.

Qualified Individual with a Disability (aka qualified handicapped individual)　　Individual with a disability (handicap) who, with or without reasonable accommodation or modification to rules, policies, practices, removal of architectural, transportation or communication barriers or provision of auxiliary services meets the essential eligibility requirements for a program/service/job.

Readily Achievable　　Easily accomplishable and able to be carried out without much difficulty or expense.

Reasonable Accommodation　　Those modifications and aids with which an otherwise qualified person with a disability could do a particular job, e.g. making existing facilities accessible, job restructuring, part-time or modified work schedules, reassignment, acquisition/modification of equipment or devices, adjustment or modification of examinations, training materials or policies, provision of a reader or interpreter. Excludes those accommodations which would impose an undue hardship on the operation of the business of the employer.

Reasonable Modifications	Those changes in policies, practices, or procedures to public accommodations that are necessary to afford the goods, services, facilities, privileges, advantages, or accommodations to the individual with disabilities. Excludes those modifications which would fundamentally alter the nature of the goods, services, facilities, privileges, advantages and accommodations.
Recipient	An entity, including state/local government, business or an individual, provided a grant, loan, or contract, for funds, services, or property.
Rehabilitation Act (Rehab Act)	A basic federal law containing funded programs and civil rights for persons with disabilities.
Special Ed	Education for a child with a disability, including related services, under EAHCA (now IDEA) and state/local laws.
TAB	Temporarily Able-Bodied.
TDD	Telecommunications Device for the Deaf (see also TTY). It uses graphic communications in transmission of coded signals through a wire or radio communication system.
Telecommunications Relay System	Telephone transmission service that allows a hearing or speech impaired person to communicate by wire or radio with an unimpaired person in a manner that is functionally equivalent to regular voice communications or radio for hearing services.

TTY	Mechanical device which persons use to type out their conversation and thus communicate. Commonly used to communicate with persons who are hearing impaired. Former usage more frequently was TDD.
UFAS	Uniform Federal Accessibility Standard.
UMTA	Urban Mass Transit Administration, part of DOT.
Undue Hardship	An action requiring significant difficulty or expense.
Washington Mentality	Total disability. Loss of vision beyond the Potomac River. Loss of ability to hear and/or understand what people say. Inability to be mobile, except to warm climates in bad weather or on other junkets (see also "Bureaucrat").
White Cane Law	State law with criminal sanction prohibiting discrimination against persons with physical disabilities or who are blind in employment, places of public accommodation, or housing.

BY THE NUMBERS

No compilation would be complete without highlighting certain numbers which have been so ingrained in the disability dialogue as not to need words to buttress/clutter their meaning. Herewith:

16(a)	Section 16(a) of the Urban Mass Transit Act (special efforts for handicapped and elderly persons).
501	Section 501 of the Rehab Act (nondiscrimination/affirmative action by federal government).
502	Section 502 of the Rehab Act (ATBCB).
503	Section 503 of the Rehab Act (affirmative action).
504	Section 504 of the Rehab Act (nondiscrimination).
43,000,000	The most commonly accepted number of persons with disabilities in the United States.
A117.1	The number of the ANSI standard for accessibility of buildings.
P.L. 90-480	ABA.
P.L. 94-142	EAHCA.
P.L. 101-336	ADA.
42 U.S.C.Sec.12101 Note et seq.	ADA.
Title V	Title V of the Rehab Act.
29 U.S.C. Sec. 791 et seq.	Sections 501 et *seq.*

STATE BY STATE GUIDE: LAWS AND CONTACTS

The next several pages contain an enumeration of laws and points of contact. Codes were reviewed to ascertain anti-discrimination mandates in employment, housing, public accommodations, and education. These are cited to the state law. Notation is made of the persons who are protected, i.e., "physical" for persons with physical disabilities and "mental" for persons with mental disabilities.

Where there is a blank space it means that no law was found in the particular subject area for the particular jurisdiction. Program funding statutes, such as state education laws which implement the Individuals with Disabilities Education Act (Chapter 5) are not noted. Only traditional nondiscrimination, civil rights, White Cane, and accessibility laws are identified.

The nondiscrimination mandates, statutory provisions or administrative interpretations of laws with regard to Acquired Immune Deficiency Syndrome (AIDS) are also noted. AIDS laws refer to persons with AIDS, AIDS Related Complex and HIV +. This is an issue of increasing importance. AIDS laws are often a corollary of laws affecting disabled persons. The administrative materials identified here relating to AIDS are interpretations of laws prohibiting discrimination against disabled persons. (Contacts for information on AIDS are in Appendix III.)

Because the definition of "employer" varies from state to state, this definition should be checked carefully. Commonly, an "employer" includes any person, state, or political subdivision employing the requisite number of employees for each working day in 20 or more calendar weeks. Generally any person acting directly or indirectly as an agent of a qualified employer is also included. The minimum number of employees an "employer" must have in order to fall under the state's particular definition appears in parentheses after references to the scope of state protection.

Common exceptions to state definitions of "employer" include an exclusively social club, or a fraternal, charitable, educational, or religious non-profit organization or association. The United States and any company wholly owned by the federal government as well as Indian Tribes are also exempted from state laws. Definitions in state laws also generally exclude an employer's parents, spouse, children, and domestic servants who work in and around the employer's household.

White Cane laws are also noted. These are laws which prohibit discrimination against blind and vision impaired (and, in recent years, other physically disabled) persons in employment. These laws also quite commonly prohibit discrimination in places of public accommodation such as hotels, inns, restaurants, train stations, as well as other places to which the public in general is invited. The definition of place of public accommodation in state law should be checked carefully. In certain states that definition is broad enough to embrace discrimination in housing and education. White Cane laws are characterized by criminal, not civil, sanctions. This means the state law enforcement office, the State Attorney General, unless delegated to a local official, is the entity to initiate legal proceedings to redress alleged discrimination. The White Cane law may be indicated as the only statutory protection or it may be listed in conjunction with other statutes. White Cane laws also typically prohibit extra charges being imposed for an individual's guide dog, though the dog's owner is responsible for any damage the dog may cause.

Where a state has a law which prohibits discrimination in a particular category, but disabled persons are not protected by that law, the word "No" is utilized and the citation to the law given. This means there is no protection for persons with disabilities under that law.

In the area of accessibility, there are citations to the basic state public accommodation laws and state codes on access, as well as indication of the scope of their application. "Public" and "publicly owned or funded" buildings may include state/locally government owned or funded structures. "Private" buildings may include places of potential employment as well as structures to which the general populace, including persons with disabilities, is invited, may work or visit. Readers must note that both categories are subject to idiosyncratic nuances in the law's coverage and exceptions that are indigenous to the particular state. The standard of accessibility utilized in the state is also noted. These are standards to use in connection with the checklists in Chapters 3 and 4, relating to accessibility and housing.

The listing of states also contains at least one address and telephone number to contact in each state for information. If the people there do not know the answer to a question, they should be able to refer callers to other people who can be more responsive.

CAVEAT: These citations and contacts are current as of January, 1991. The laws as well as contacts are always subject to change and updating. Since the first edition that has been especially true with regard to provisions relating to AIDS.

STATE LAWS AND CONTACTS

ALABAMA

Employment–Public employment only. Physical. ALA. Code 21-7-8. Policy Statement. ALA. Code 21-7-1
AIDS–
Public Accommodations–White Cane Law only. ALA. Code 21-7-3
Housing–Physical. ALA. Code 21-7-9
Education–
Accessibility–Buildings used by the public or constructed with government funds. ANSI A117.1-1961/71 and Alabama. ALA. Code 21-4-1
Contact–Governor's Committee on Employment of the Handicapped
Division of Rehabilitation & Crippled Children
Post Office Box 11586
2129 East South Boulevard
Montgomery, Alabama 36111-0586
(205) 281-8750

ALASKA

Employment–Physical. Mental. (1)ALASKA Stat. 18.80.220
Public Funded. ALASKA Stat. 47.80.010
AIDS–
Public Accommodations–Physical. Mental. ALASKA Stat. 18.80.200
Public funded. ALASKA Stat. 47.80.010.
White Cane Law. ALASKA Stat. 18.06.020.
Housing–Physical. Mental. ALASKA Stat. 18.80.240
Public Funded ALASKA Stat. 47.80.010
Education–Not covered. ALASKA Stat. 18.80.010
Public funded. ALASKA Stat. 47.80.010
Accessibility–Public. ANSI A117.1-1980 and ALASKA
ALASKA Stat. 35.10.015

Alaska Cotinued
Contact–Governor's Committee on Employment of the
  Handicapped
  Commissioner's Office–DOL
  Post Office Box 7-018
  Anchorage, Alaska 99510
  (907) 264-2400
State Commission for Human Rights
  800 A Street, Suite 202
  Anchorage, Alaska 99501
  (907) 276-7474

ARIZONA

Employment–Physical. (15) ARIZ. Rev.Stat. 41-1463
AIDS–Covered. ARIZ. Rev. Stat. 41-1461
Public Accommodation–Not covered. ARIZ. Rev. Stat. 41-1442
  White Cane Law 24-411
Housing–
Education–
Accessibility–Public. Private.
Coverage of alterations to structures expanded after January
1987
ANSI A117.1-1980 and Arizona
ARIZ. Rev. Stat. 34-401
Contact–Governor's Committee on Employment of the
  Handicapped
  1535 West Jefferson
  Phoenix, Arizona 85007
  (602) 543-3850
Civil Rights Division
  1275 West Jefferson Street
  Phoenix, Arizona 85005
  (602)542-5263
Governor's Office of Affirmative Action
  1700 West Washington Street
  State Capitol, Room 804
  Phoenix, Arizona 85007
  (602)542-3711

ARKANSAS

Employment–Public employment–Physical. ARK. Stat. Ann.
82-2901

Arkansas continued
AIDS–
*Public Accommodations–*White Cane Law. ARK. Stat. Ann.
82-2902
*Housing–*White Cane Law. ARK. Stat. Ann. 82-2905
Education–
*Accessibility–*Publicly owned or funded
ATBCB-1981 and Arkansas
ARK. Stat. Ann. 14-627
Contact–Governor's Commission on People with Disabilities
7th & Main Streets
P.O. Box 3781
Little Rock Arkansa 72203
(501) 682-6695 or 371-1654 (Voice)
(501) 371-1656 (TDD)

CALIFORNIA

*Employment–*Physical. Medical Condition. (5) CAL. Code
Government Sec. 12940
CAL. Civil Code 54.5
*AIDS–*CAL. Health and Safety Code. Sec. 199.20
Sec.199.81 et seq.
*Public Accommodations–*Physical. CAL. Civil Code 51.5, 54.1-54.3
*Housing–*Yes. Within definition of Public accommodation, CAL.
Civil Code 54.1-54.3
Not within CAL. Code Government Sec.12955
*Education–*Physical. Public and Private. CAL. Civil Code Secs.
51.5, 54.3. State Funded Post Secondary Education. CAL.
Code Education Sec. 67.310.
Community Colleges see CAL. Code Education Secs. 72011
and 78440
*Accessibility–*Public. Private.
California.
CAL. Code Government Sec. 4450
Contact– Governor's Committee on Employment of Disabled
Persons
P.O. Box 942880, MIC 41
Sacramento California 94280-0001
(916) 323-2545 (voice or TDD)

California continued
Department of Fair Employment and Housing
2014 "T" Street
Sacramento, California 95814-6835
(916) 739-4621

COLORADO

Employment–Physical. Mental. (1) (state employment) 4CCR
801-1.Physical. (1) (Private) COLO. Rev. Stat. 24-34-402.
Mental as of 7/1/92
White Cane Law. COLO. Rev. Stat. 24-34-801
AIDS–Covered. Civil Rights Commission 3/22/86
Public Accommodations–Physical. COLO. Rev. Stat. 24-34-602
Mental as of 7/1/90
White Cane Law. COLO. Rev. Stat. 24-34-801
Housing–Physical. COLO. Rev. Stat. 24-34-502
Mental as of 7/1/90
Education–Within definition of place of public accommodations.
COLO. Rev. Stat. 24-34-602
Physical. Mental as of 7/1/92.
Accessibility–Public. Private.
Colorado
COLO. Rev. Stat. 9-5-101 et seq.
Contact– Colorado Coalition for Citizens with Disabilities
789 Sherman Street, Suite 520
Denver CO 80203
(303) 863-0113 or 863-0116 (Voice)
(303) 861-2735 (TDD)
Colorado Civil Rights Commission
Room 600c, State Services Building
1525 Sherman Street
Denver Colorado 80203
(303) 866-2621 or 866-2624

CONNECTICUT

Employment–Physical. Mental. Mentally Retarded. Learning
Disability (3)CONN. Gen. Stat. Ann. 46a-60
AIDS–Covered. Human Rights Commission Policy Letter 7/86
Testing & Disclosure: P.L. 89-246 (1989)
Public Accommodation–Physical. Mental. Mentally Retarded.
Learning Disability.
CONN. Gen. Stat. Ann. 46a-64.

Connecticut continued

Housing–Physical. Mentally Retarded. Mental. Learning
Disability (within definition of place of public
accommodation). CONN. Gen. Stat. Ann. 46a-64

Education–Mentally Retarded. Learning Disability. Physical.
CONN. Gen. Stat. 46a-75

Accessibility–Public. Private.
ANSI A117.1-1961 and Connecticut.
CONN. Gen. Stat. 29-269 to 29-274.

Contact– Governor's Committee on Employment of the
Handicapped
Department of Labor Building
200 Folly Brook Boulevard
Wethersfield CT 06109
(203) 566-8061.

Commission on Human Rights and Opportunities
90 Washington Street
Hartford, Connecticut 06106
(203) 566-3350, 566-4895

*Also note: Conn. Constitution, Article 21, amending Article 5 prohibits
the denial of equal protection of laws, discrimination and segregation
based on physical or mental disability.

DELAWARE

Employment–Physical. Mental. (20) DEL. Code Ann. 19-724.

AIDS–Testing and Confidentiality. DEL. Code Ann. 16-1201 et
seq.

Public Accommodations–White Cane Law. DEL. Code Ann
9-2903

Housing–Physical. Mental. DEL. Code 6-4601

Accessibility–Publicly owned, funded, leased, altered
ANSI A117.1-1980 and Delaware.
DEL. Code Ann. 29-7303

Contact–Governor's Committee on Employment of People with
Disabilities
Delaware Ellwyn Building
321 East 11th Street
Wilmington, Delaware 19801
(302)577-3915

Delaware continued
Human Relations Commission
Williams Service Center
820 North French Street
Wilmington, Delaware 19801
(302)577-3716
Department of Labor
Anti-Discrimination Section
820 North French Street
Wilmington, Delaware 19801
(302) 577-2900

DISTRICT OF COLUMBIA

Employment-Physical. Mental. (1) D.C. Code Ann. 1-2512
White Cane Law. D.C. Code Ann. 6-1504
AIDS-Covered. Opinion of Corporation Counsel (10/15/85)
Office of Human Rights Policy Statement
10/9/86; D.C. Code Ann. 6-2801 et seq.
Public Accommodations-Physical. Mental. D.C. Code Ann.
1-2519
White Cane Law. D.C. Code Ann. 6-1501
Housing-Physical. Mental. D.C. Code Ann. 1-2515
White Cane Law. D.C. Code Ann. 6-1505
Education-Physical. Mental. D.C. Code Ann. 1-2520
Accessibility-Public. Private.
District of Columbia. BOCA. ANSI A117.1-1980.
D.C. Code Ann. 6-1703, D.C.M.R. 512A
Contact-Mayor's Committee on Handicapped Individuals
605 "G" Street, NW
Washington, D.C. 20001
(202) 727-4034
Office of Human Rights
2000-14th Street, NW
Washington, D.C. 20009
(202) 939-8740 (Voice)
(202)939-8793 (TDD)

FLORIDA

Employment-Physical. Mental Retardation. Developmental
Disability. AIDS (15) FLA. Stat. Ann.760. 22
White Cane Law. FLA. Stat. Ann. 413.08
1988 Florida Laws No. 380 Sec. 45 (7/6/88)

Florida continued
AIDS–Covered. FLA. Stat. Ann. 381.606
    1988 Florida Laws No. 380 Sec. 45 (7/6/88)
    FLA. Stat. Ann. 760.50; Case law; Policy Memoranda 1985-86.
Public Accommodations–White Cane Law. FLA. Stat. Ann. 413.08
Housing–Physical. AIDS FLA. Stat. Ann. 760.23
    1988 Florida Laws No. 380 Sec. 45 (7/6/88)
    White Cane Law. FLA. Stat. Ann. 413.08
Education–"Handicap." FLA. Stat. Ann. 228.2001
    AIDS in federally funded.
    Florida Laws No. 380 Sec. 45 (7/6/88)
Accessibility–Publicly owned or build on its behalf used by the
    public
    ANSI A117.1-1980.
    FLA. Stat. Ann. 255.21
Contact–Governor's Employment Alliance for Employment of
    Disabled Citizens
    Sun Federal Place
    345 South Magnolia Drive, Suite A-17
    Tallahassee, Florida 32301-2947
    (904) 487-2222 (Voice)
    (904) 487-0925 (TDD)
Commission on Human Relations
    325 John Knox Road
    Building F Suite 240
    Tallahassee, Florida 32303-1570
    (904) 488-7082
    (800) 342-8170

GEORGIA

Employment–Physical. Mental. (15) GA. Code Ann. 45-19-22
    GA. Code Ann. 34-6A-1
AIDS–Confidentiality of testing. GA. Code Ann. 24-9-47
Public Accommodations–White Cane Law. GA. Code Ann. 30-4-1
Housing–No. GA. Code Ann. 8-3-202
    White Cane Law. GA. Code Ann. 30-4-2
Education–
Accessibility–Public. Private.
    ANSI A117.1-1986 and Georgia.
    GA. Code Ann. 30-3.2

Georgia continued
Contact–Governor's Committee on Employment of Handicapped
Persons
878 Peachstree Street, N.E.
7th Floor
Atlanta, Georgia 30309
(404) 894-7552
Office of Fair Employment Practices
156 Trinity Ave, SW
Atlanta, Georgia 30303
(404) 656-1736
Governor's Council on Human Relations
State Capitol
Atlanta, Georgia 30334
(404) 656-6757

HAWAII

*Employment–*Physical. Mental. (1)HAWAII Rev. Stat. Tit. 21, Ch.
378
*AIDS–*Hawaii AIDS Law: Confidentiality of Records. Housing,
employment, education. HAWAII Rev. Stat. 325-101 et seq.
HAWAII Rev. Stat. 515-3; Penalty for Disclosure P.A. 377
*Public Accommodations–*White Cane Law. HAWAII. Rev. Stat.
347-13
*Housing–*Physical. HAWAII. Rev. Stat. 515-1 et seq.
Education–
*Accessibility–*Public.
Latest ANSI-A117.1 and Hawaii.
HAWAII. Rev. Stat. Title 9, Sec. 103.50
Contact–Commission on Persons with Disabilities
500 Ala Moana Boulevard.
5 Waterford Plaza-Room 210
Honolulu, Hawaii 96813
(808) 548-7606
Department of Commerce and Consumer Affairs
1010 Richards Street
Honolulu, Hawaii 96812
(808) 548-4565, 548-3976

Hawaii *continued*
Department of Labor and Industrial Relations
  Enforcement Division
  830 Punchbowl Street
  Honolulu, Hawaii 96813
  (808) 548-7625, 548-7508

IDAHO

Employment–Physical. Mental. (10)
  IDAHO Code 67-5909
AIDS–Testing. IDAHO Code 39-5408
Public Accommodations–No. IDAHO Code 67-5909
  White Cane Law. IDAHO Code 18-5812
Housing–No. IDAHO Code 67-5909
Education–No. IDAHO Code 67-5909
Accessibility–Public owned or funded.
  ANSI as amended and IDAHO.
  IDAHO Code Title 39 Sec. 3201
Contact–Governor's Committee on Employment of People With
  Disabilities
  317 Main Street
  Boise, Idaho 83735
  (208) 334-6193
Commission on Human Rights
  450 West State Street
  Boise, Idaho 83720
  (208) 334-2873

ILLINOIS

Employment–Physical. Mental. (1) ILL. Rev.Stat. 68-2-103
  ILL. Const. Art.1, Sec. 19
AIDS–*Confidentiality. ILL.Rev.Stat..111 1/2 Sec. 7301 et seq., ILL.
  Department Public Health Rules Part 697; P.A. 86-902 (1989);
  Opinion of Legal Counsel (6/86)*
Public Accommodations–Physical. Mental. ILL. Rev.Stat. 68-5-102
  White Cane Law. ILL. Rev. Stat. Code 23-3363
Housing–Physical. Mental. ILL. Rev. Stat. 68-3-102
  ILL. Const. Art. 1, Sec. 19
Education–No. ILL. Rev. Stat. 111-1208

Illinois continued
Accessibility–Public. Private.
  Illinois (relies heavily on ANSI A117.1-1980).
  ILL. Rev. Stat. 111 1/2 Sec. 3711
Contact–Illinois Jobs Committee For The Handicapped
  Room 100, State Capital
  Springfield, Illinois 62706
  (217) 782-3212
  (312) 814-2922 (Voice), 814-3040 (TDD)
Department of Human Rights
  100 West Randolph Street, Suite 10-100
  Chicago, Illinois 60601
  (312) 814-6200, 814-6245

INDIANA

Employment–Physical. Mental. (6) IND. Code Ann. 22-9-1-3
  White Cane Law. IND. Code Ann. 16-7-5-6
  State Employment IND. Code Ann. 4-15-12-2
AIDS–Testing: IND. Code Ann. 16-9-9.5 et seq.
Public Accommodations–Physical. Mental. IND. Code Ann.
  22-9-1-3
  White Cane Law. IND. Code Ann. 16-7-5-2
Housing–Physical. Mental. IND. Code Ann. 22-9-1-3
  White Cane Law. IND. Code Ann. 16-7-5.5-2
Education–Physical. Mental. IND. Code Ann. 22-9-1-3
Accessibility–Public. Private.
  Indiana.
  IND. Code Ann. 22-11-1-17
Contact–State Commission for the Handicapped
  P.O. Box 1964
  1330 W. Michigan Street
  Indianapolis, Indiana 46206-1964
  (317) 633-0288
Civil Rights Commission
  32 East Washington Street
  Indianapolis, Indiana 46204-2773
  (317) 232-2600, 232-2612, 232-1987

IOWA

Employment–Physical. Mental. AIDS, HIV, ARC. (4) IOWA
  Code Ann. 601A.6
  White Cane Law. IOWA Code Ann. 601D.2

Iowa continued

AIDS–Covered: IOWA Code Ann. 601A.2
Testing. IOWA Code Ann. 1351.1 et seq.
Public Accommodations–Physical. Mental. AIDS, HIV, ARC.
IOWA Code Ann. 601A.7
White Cane Law. IOWA Code Ann. 601D.4, 601D.11.
Housing–Physical. Mental. AIDS, HIV, ARC. IOWA Code Ann.
601A.8
Education–Physical. Mental. AIDS, HIV, ARC. IOWA Code
Ann. 601A.9
Accessibility–Public. Private.
ANSI A117.1-1980 and Iowa.
IOWA Code Ann. 104A
Contact–Iowa Commission of Persons with Disabilities
Department of Human Rights
Lucas State Office Building
Des Moines, Iowa 50319
(515) 281-5969
Civil Rights Commission
211 East Maple Street
Grimes State Office Building
Des Moines, Iowa 50319
(515) 281-4121, (800) 457-4416

KANSAS

Employment–Physical. (4) KAN. Stat. 44-1009
AIDS–Kansas Infectious Disease Act: Confidentiality and
Reporting, KAN. Stat. Ann. 65-128
Covered case law.
Public Accommodations–Physical. KAN. Stat. Ann. 44-1009
White Cane Law. KAN. Stat. Ann. 39-1101
Housing–No. KAN. Stat. Ann. 44-1016
Education–Physical. Public Institutions KAN. Stat. Ann. 44-1009
Accessibility–Public. Private.
ANSI A117.1-1980 and Kansas.
KAN. Stat. Ann. Ch. 13 Sec. 58-1301
Contact–Kansas Commission on Disability Concerns
1430 S. Topeka Avenue
Topeka, Kansas 66612
(913) 232-1722 (Voice)
(913) 296-5044 (TDD)

Kansas *continued*
Commission on Civil Rights
Landon State Office Building
900 SW Jackson, 8th Floor, Suite 851 South
Topeka, Kansas 66612
(913) 296-3206

KENTUCKY

Employment-Physical. KY. Rev. Stat. 207.130
Affirmative Action Plan (1988), KY. Rev. Stats. Ch.18A.
AIDS-No. Communicable disease exception: KY. Rev. Stat.
207.130-207.240.
Public Accommodations-No. KY. Rev. Stat. 344.120
White Cane Law. KY. Rev. Stat. 258.500
Housing-Physical. KY. Rev. Stat. 207.180
Education-
Accessibility-Public and Private.
ANSI A117.1-1980 and Kentucky.
KY. Rev. Stat. 198.50
Contact-Committee on Employment of the Handicapped
600 West Cedar
Louisville, Kentucky 40203
(502) 588-4073
Commission on Human Rights
701 West Muhammad Ali Boulevard
Louisville, Kentucky 40203
(502) 588-4024

LOUISIANA

Employment-Physical. Psychological, Mental Retardation,
Mental Disorder. (15) 46 LA. Rev. Stat. Ann. 2254
AIDS-
Public Accommodations-White Cane Law. 46 LA. Rev. Stat.
Ann. Secs. 1952, 1954
Housing-Physical. Mental. 46 LA. Rev. Stat. Ann. 2254
White Cane Law. 46 LA Rev. Stat. Ann. 1953
Education-Physical. Mental. 46 LA. Rev. Stat. Ann. 1954
Accessibility-Public. Private.
ANSI 1977 (sic. 1980) and Louisiana.
40 LA. Rev. Stat. Ann. 1731 et seq.

Louisiana continued
  Contact–Division of Vocational Rehabilitation
    P.O. Box 94371
    1755 Florida Boulevard
    Baton Rouge, Louisiana 70804
    (504) 342-2719

MAINE

Employment–Physical. Mental. (1) 5 ME Rev. Stat. Ann. 4551 et
  seq.
  White Cane Law. 17 ME. Rev. Stat. Ann. 1311.
AIDS–Covered. Human Relations Commission Policy statement
  3/86.
  Testing and limited disclosure:
  5 ME. Rev. Stat. Ann. 17001 et seq.
  Employment: 5 ME. Rev. Stat. Ann.19201
Public Accommodations–Physical. Mental. 5 ME. Rev. Stat.
  Ann.4591 et seq.
  White Cane Law. 17 ME. Rev. Stat. Ann.1311, 17 ME. Rev.
  Stat. Ann. 1312
Housing–Physical. Mental. 5 ME Rev. Stat. Ann. 4581
Education–Physical. Mental 5 ME. Rev. Stat. Ann. 4601
Accessibility–Public. Private.
  ANSI A117.1-1986 and Maine.
  25 ME. Rev. Stat. Ann. 2701 et seq.
  Contact–Governor's Committee on Employment of the
    Handicapped
    32 Winthrop Street
    Augusta, Maine 04330
    (207) 289-3485
  Human Rights Commission
    State House-Station 51
    Augusta, Maine 04333
    (207) 289-2326

MARYLAND

Employment–Physical. Mental. (15) MD. Ann. Code Art. 49B
  Sec. 3
  White Cane Law. MD. Ann. Code Art. 30 Sec. 33

Maryland continued
AIDS–Employment, Public Accommodations, Housing: Covered under MD. Ann. Code Art. 14 Sec. 3.
Maryland Human Relations Commission. Regs 4/88
COMAR 14.03.02; Opinion of Legal Counsel 11/86
Public Accommodations–Physical. Mental. MD. Ann. Code Art. 49B Sec. 8
White Cane Law. MD. Ann. Code Art. 30 Sec. 33
Housing–Physical. Mental. MD. Ann. Code. Art. 49B Sec. 20
White Cane Law. MD. Ann. Code Art. 30 Sec. 33
Education–Physical. MD Ann. Code. Art. 6 Sec. 105
Accessibility–Public. Private.
ANSI A117.1-1980 and Maryland.
MD. Ann. Code Art. 41 Sec. 257JK
Contact–Governor's Committee on Employment of the Handicapped
1 Market Center, P.O. Box 10
300 West Lexington
Baltimore, Maryland 21201
(301) 333-2264 (Voice) (301) 333-3098 (TDD)
Commission on Human Relations
20 East Franklin Street
Baltimore, Maryland 21202
(301) 333-1700, 333-1715

MASSACHUSETTS

Employment–Physical. Mental. (6) MASS. Ann. Laws 151B Sec. 4
AIDS–Covered. Commission Against Discrimination Policy Statement 1/86. Guidelines 9/86. Case law.
Testing in employment. MASS. Ann. Laws 111 Sec. 70F
Public Accommodations–Physical. Mental. MASS. Ann. Laws 272 Secs. 98, 98A
White Cane Law. MASS. Ann. Laws Sec. 92A
MASS. Ann. Laws Ch. 151,Sec. 5
Housing–Blind. Hearing Impaired. MASS. Ann. Laws 151B Sec. 6
Education–Blind. Deaf. MASS. Ann. Laws 151c Sec. 2(e)
Accessibility–Public. Private.
Massachusetts.
MASS. Ann. Laws 22 Sec. 13A, 143 Sec. 3W

Massachusetts *continued*
    *Also note: MASS. Constitutional Amendment Art. 114 prohibiting dis-
    crimination against handicapped individuals in a program or activity
    within the Commonwealth.

Contact–Commission on Employment of the Handicapped
    Department of Employment and Training
    19 Stanford Street, 4th Floor
    Boston, Massachusetts 02146
    (617) 727-1826
Commission Against Discrimination
    1 Ashburton Place
    Boston, Massachusetts 02108
    (617) 727-3990

MICHIGAN

Employment–Physical. Mental. (1) MICH. Stat. Ann.37.1202
AIDS–Policy Statement covering employment, housing, public
    accommodations, education. 8/15/86.
    Confidentiality Act. MICH. Stat. Ann. 333.1101, Secs. 5131
    and 5133, P.A. 271 (1989)
    P.A. 174 (1989)
    Penalties for Disclosure: P.A. 271 and 174 (1989).
Public Accommodations–Physical. Mental. MICH. Stat. Ann.
    37.1302
    White Cane Law. MICH. Stat. Ann. 750.502c
Housing–Physical. Mental. MICH. Stat. Ann. 37.1502
    White Cane Law. MICH. Stat. Ann. 750.502c
Education–Physical. Mental. MICH. Stat Ann. 37.1402
    White Cane Law. MICH. Stat. Ann. 750.502c
Accessibility–Public. Private.
    ANSI A117.1-1961/71 and Michigan.
    MICH. Stat. Ann.125.1351 et seq.
Contact–Commission on Handicapped Concerns
    Box 30015
    309 North Washington Avenue
    Lansing, Michigan 48909
    (517) 373-8397 (Voice/TDD)
Department of Civil Rights
    1200 Sixth Street
    Detroit, Michigan 48226
    (313) 256-2615, 256-2578, 256-2663

Michigan continued
Department of Civil Rights
303 W. Kalamazoo
Lansing, Michigan 48913
(517) 334-6079

MINNESOTA

Employment–Physical. Mental. (1) MINN. Stat. Ann. 363.03
White Cane Law MINN. Stat. Ann. 256C.01
AIDS–Covered. Gov. Exec. Order 12/86 State employees 12/86.
Also case law.
Public Accommodations–Physical. Mental. MINN. Stat. Ann.
363.03
White Cane Law. MINN. Stat. Ann. 256C.02
Housing–Physical. Mental. MINN. Stat. Ann. 363.03
White Cane Law. MINN. Stat. Ann. 256C.025
Education–Physical. Mental. MINN. Stat. Ann. 363.03
Accessibility–Public. Private.
ANSI A117.1-1961/71 and Minnesota. MINN. Stat. Ann.
471.465 et seq.
Contact–State Council on Disability
145 Metro Square Building
7th & Jackson Streets
St. Paul, Minnesota 55101
(612) 296-6785
(800) 652-9747
Department of Human Rights
5th Floor Bremer Tower
Seventh Place at Minnesota Street
St. Paul, Minnesota 55101
(612) 296-5663, 296-5665

MISSISSIPPI

Employment–Physical. State employment only. MISS. Code Ann.
25-9-149
White Cane Law. MISS. Code Ann. 43-6-15
AIDS–State employees. MISS. Code Ann. 25-9-149
Public Accommodations–White Cane Law. MISS. Code Ann.
43-6-5
Housing–White Cane Law. MISS. Code Ann. 43-6-3 ("public
facilities")
Education–

Mississippi continued
Accessibility–Public owned or funded.
    ANSI A117.1-1980. UFAS. Mississippi.
    MISS. Code Ann. 43-6-101
    Contact–Governor's Office of Handicapped Services
    Department. of Rehabilitation Services
    P.O. Box 22806
    Jackson, Mississippi 39225
    (601) 354-6100

MISSOURI

Employment–Physical. Mental. AIDS. (6) MO. Ann. Stat. Sec.
    213.055 . MO. Ann. Stat. 191.665
    White Cane Law MO. Ann. Stat. 209.180
AIDS–Testing and Confidentiality: Missouri AIDS Act. MO.
    Ann. Stat. 191.650 et seq.
    Covered. Commission on Human Rights Policy Statement 6/86
Public Accommodations–Physical. Mental. AIDS. MO. Ann. Stat.
    Sec. 213.065
    White Cane Law.: visual, hearing, or physical disabilities. MO.
    Ann. Stat. Secs. 209.150
Housing–Physical. Mental. AIDS. MO. Ann. Stat. Sec.
    213.040–MO. Ann. Stat. 213.050, MO. Ann. Stat. 191.665
Education–Physical. Mental. Within MO. Ann. Stat. 213.065
    public accommodations. AIDS MO. Ann. Stat. 191.665
Accessibility–Publicly owned or funded.
    ANSI A117.1-1961/71 and Missouri.
    MO. Ann. Stat. Sec. 8.610 et seq.
    Contact–Governor's Committee on Employment of People with
    Disabilities
    Box 1668
    3315 West Truman Boulevard
    Jefferson, City Missouri 65102
    (314) 751-2600 (Voice or TDD)
    Commission on Human Rights
    3315 W. Truman Boulevard
    P.O. Box 1129
    Jefferson City, Missouri 65102-1129
    (314) 751-3325

MONTANA

Employment–Physical. Mental. (1) MONT. Code Ann. 49-2-303
White Cane Law. MONT. Code Ann. 49-4-202
AIDS–
Public Accommodations–Physical. Mental. MONT. Code Ann.
49-2-304
White Cane Law. MONT. Code Ann. 49-4-211
Housing–Physical. Mental. MONT. Code Ann. 49-2-305
White Cane Law. MONT. Code Ann. 49-4-212
Education–Physical. Mental. MONT. Code Ann. 49-2-307
Accessibility–Public.
UFAS and Montana.
MONT. Code Ann. 50-60-201
Contact–Governor's Committee on Employment of People with
Disabilities
Personnel Division
Mitchell Building, Room 130
Helena, Montana 59520
(406) 444-3871/444-3886
Department of Labor and Industry
Human Rights Division
P.O. Box 1728
1236 6th Avenue
Helena, Montana 59624-1728
(406) 444-3870, 444-2884

NEBRASKA

Employment–Physical. Mental. (1 for publically funded & 15 for
private employment) 48 NEB. Rev. Stat. 131
AIDS–Covered: Employment, Public Accommodation, Housing,
Education. 20 NEB. Rev. Stat. 167
Public Accommodations–White Cane Law. 20 NEB. Rev. Stat. 129
Housing–No. 20 NEB. Rev. Stat. 105
White Cane Law. 20 NEB. Rev. Stat. 131
Education–
Accessibility–Public. Private.
ANSI A117.1-1961/71 and Nebraska.
72 NEB. Rev. Stat. 1101

Nebraska continued
  Contact–Governor's Committee on Employment of the
     Handicapped
     Nebraska Job Service, Department of Labor
     P.O. Box 94600
     550 South 16th Street
     Lincoln, NE 68509
     (402) 471-8451
  Equal Opportunity Commission
     P.O. Box 94934
     301 Centennial Mall South
     Lincoln, Nebraska 68509
     (402) 471-2024

NEVADA

Employment–Physical. Aural. Visual. (15) NEV. Rev. Stat. 613.330
AIDS–
Public Accommodations–White Cane Law. NEV. Rev. Stat.
     651.070
     Protection extends to physically, as well as visually and aurally
     handicapped: NEV. Rev. Stat. 651.070.
Housing–No. NEV. Rev. Stat. 118.100
     Dogs for blind, deaf and physically handicapped persons.
     NEV. Rev. Stat. 118.105
Education–Within definition of place of public accommodation in
     White Cane Law.
     NEV. Rev. Stat. 651.050
Accessibility–Publicly owned or funded.
     ATBCB-1982.
     NEV. Rev. Stat. 338.180
  Contact–Governor's Committee on Employment of People with
     Disabilities
     3100 Mill International, Suite 115
     Reno, Nevada 89502
     (702) 789-0336
  Equal Rights Commission
     1515 East Tropicana
     Las Vegas, Nevada 89158
     (702) 486-7161

NEW HAMPSHIRE

Employment–Physical. Mental. (6) N.H. Rev. Stat. Ann. 354-A
   White Cane Law. N.H. Rev. Stat. Ann. 167-C:5
AIDS–Covered. Commission on Human Rights Policy Letter 6/86.
   AIDS Confidentiality Act: Testing and Confidentiality N.H.
   Rev. Stat. 141-F
   Board of Education Guidelines for School Employees N.H.
   Rev. Stat. Ann. 141F:1
Public Accommodations–Physical. Mental. N.H. Rev. Stat. Ann.
   354-A
   White Cane Law. N.H. Rev. Stat. Ann. 167-C:2 and N.H. Rec.
   Stat. Ann. 167-D.
Housing–Physical. Mental. N.H. Rev. Stat. Ann. 354-A
Education–Physical. Mental. N.H. Rev. Stat. Ann. 354-A
Accessibility–Public.
   New Hampshire.
   N.H. Rev. Stat. Ann. 155:8-a, 275-C:10
Contact–Governor's Commission for the Handicapped
   57 Regional Drive
   Concord, New Hampshire 03301
   (603) 271-2773
Commission on Human Rights
   163 Loudon Road
   Concord, New Hampshire 03301
   (603) 271-2767

NEW JERSEY

Employment–Physical. Mental. (1) N.J. Rev. Stat. 10:5
   White Cane Law. N.J. Rev. Stat. 10:5:29
AIDS–Education Program, N.J. Rev. Stat. 26:5c
   Covered: Policy Announcement 3/86; case law.
Public Accommodations–Physical. Mental. N.J. Rev. Stat. 10:5
   White Cane Law. N.J. Rev. Stat. 10:5:29
Housing–Physical. Mental. N.J. Rev. Stat. 10:5
   White Cane Law. N.J. Rev. Stat. 10:5:29
Education–Physical. Mental. (Within definition of place of public
   accommodation.)
   N.J. Rev. Stat. 10:5

New Jersey continued
  Accessibility–Public. Private.
    ANSI A117.1-1980. UFAS. ATBCB-1982.
    N.J. Rev. Stat. 52:32:5
  Contact–Governor's Committee on the Disabled
    Station Plaza, Building 4, Third Floor
    Trenton, New Jersey 08625
    (609) 633-6978, 633-6959
  Division on Civil Rights
    Department on Law and Public Safety
    Headquarters Office
    1100 Raymond Boulevard
    Newark, New Jersey 07102
    (201) 648-2700

NEW MEXICO

Employment–Physical. Mental. Medical Condition.
    (4) N.M. Stat. Ann. 28-1-7
    White Cane Law. N.M. Stat. Ann. 28-7-7
  AIDS–Covered. Human Relations Commission Policy Letter 6/86
    Testing, Confidentiality, Consent.
    1989 N.M. Laws Ch. 228, 227, 6/17/89.
  Public Accommodations–Physical. Mental. N.M. Stat. Ann. 28-1-7
    White Cane Law. N.M. Stat. Ann. 28-7-3
  Housing–Physical. Mental. N.M. Stat. Ann. 28-1-7
  Education–
  Accessibility–Public.
    ANSI A117.1-1980 and New Mexico.
    N.M. Rev. Stat. 60-13-44, 15-3-7
  Governor's Committee on Concerns of the Handicapped
    Lamy Building
    491 Old Santa Fe Trail
    Santa Fe, New Mexico 87503
    (505) 827-6465
  Human Rights Commission
    1596 Pacheo St
    Santa Fe, New Mexico 87502
    (505) 827-6838

NEW YORK

Employment–Physical. Mental. Medical. (4) N.Y. Exec. Law 296
  White Cane Law. N.Y. Civil Rights Law 47-a
AIDS–Covered. Human Rights Commission Policy Statement
  12/85 and case law.
  Testing and Confidentiality. N.Y. Public Health Law Art. 27-F,
  2-1-89
Public Accommodations–Physical. Mental. Medical. N.Y. Exec.
  Law 296, White Cane Law. N.Y. Civil Rights Law 47
Housing–Physical. Mental. Medical. N.Y. Exec. Law 296
  White Cane Law. N.Y. Civil Rights Law 47
Education–Physical. Mental. Medical. N.Y. Exec. Law 296
  White Cane Law N.Y. Civil Rights Law 47
Accessibility–Public. Private.
  ANSI A117.1-1980 and New York.
  N.Y. Public Buildings Law 50
  N.Y. Transportation Law 15b
  N.Y. Civil Rights Law 45.
Contact–State Advocate for the Disabled
  Empire State Plaza
  Agency Building #1
  Albany, New York 12223
  (518) 474-2825, 473-4129
  (212) 613-4285
State Division of Human Rights
  55 West 125th Street
  New York, New York 10027
  (212) 870-8400, 870-8794, 870-8566

NORTH CAROLINA

Employment–Physical. Mental. Visual. (15) N.C. Gen. Stat.
  168A-5, 143-422.2
AIDS–State employment covered under Office of Personnel
  Rules. Title 25 NC Admin. Code 0202
  Covered: Employment, public accommodations, housing,
  public services. N.C. Gen. Stat. 130A-148.
Public Accommodations–Physical. Mental. N.C. Gen. Stat.
  168A-6.
Housing–Physical. Mental. (Limitedly within public
  accommodations.) N.C. Gen. Stat. 168A-6
  No. N.C. Gen. Stat. 41A-1

North Carolina continued
Education–Physical. Mental. N.C. Gen. Stat. 168A-7
Accessibility–Public. Private.
  ANSI A117.1-61/71 and North Carolina.
  N.C. Gen. Stat. 143-138
Contact–Governor's Advocacy Council for Persons with
  Disabilities
  1318 Dale Street
  Raleigh, North Carolina 27605
  (919) 733-9250 (Voice/TDD)
Human Relations Council
  121 West Jones Street
  Raleigh, North Carolina 27603
  (919) 733-7996
Office of Administrative Hearings
  P.O. Box Drawer 11666
  Raleigh, North Carolina 27604
  (919) 733-0431

NORTH DAKOTA

Employment–Physical. Mental. N.D. (10)
  Century Code 14-02.4
  White Cane Law-State and State Funded Employment. N.D.
  Century Code 25-13-05
AIDS–Testing and confidentiality. N.D. Century Code 23-07.5
Public Accommodations–Physical. Mental. N.D. Century Code
  14-02.4
  White Cane Law. N.D. Century Code 25-13-02
Housing–Physical. Mental. N.D. Century Code 14-02.4
Education–Physical. Mental. N.D. Century Code 14-02.4
Accessibility–Public ANSI A117.1-1961/71 and North Dakota.
  N.D. Century Code 23-13-12 and 13
Contact–Governor's Committee on Employment of People with
  Disabilities
  State Capitol Building
  3rd Floor
  Bismark, North Dakota 58505
  (701) 224-2970

North Dakota *continued*
Department of Labor
State Capitol-5th Floor
Bismarck, North Dakota 58505
(701) 224-2660

OHIO

Employment–Physical. Mental. (4) OHIO Rev. Code Sec. 4112
AIDS–Covered. Civil Rights Commission Policy Statement.
3/25/87. Also case law.
Public Accommodations–Physical. Mental. OHIO Rev. Code Sec.
4112
White Cane Law. OHIO Rev. Code Sec. 955.43
Housing–Physical. Mental. OHIO Rev. Code Sec. 4112
Education–Physical. Mental. Post-secondary education. OHIO
Rev. Code Sec. 4112
Accessibility–Public. Private.
ANSI A117.1-1980 and BOCA. OHIO Rev. Code Sec. 3781.111
Contact–Governor's Council on People with Disabilities
400 East Campus View Boulevard
Columbus, Ohio 43235-4604
(614) 438-1393
(800) 282-4536 ext. 1391
Civil Rights Commission
220 Parsons Avenue
Columbus, Ohio 43215
(614) 466-7637, 466-2785

OKLAHOMA

Employment–Physical. Mental. (15) OKLA. Stat. Ann. Title 25
Sec. 1301
Affirmative action in State Government. OKLA. Stat. Ann.
Title 74 Sec. 840
AIDS–Covered. Human Rights Comm. Policy 4/87
Public Accommodations–Physical. Mental. OKLA. Stat. Ann.
Title 25 Sec. 1402
White Cane Law. OKLA. Stat. Ann. Title 7 Sec. 19
Housing–Physical. Mental. OKLA. Stat. Ann. Title 25 Sec. 1451
Education–Physical. Mental. Within definition of places of public
accommodation. OKLA. Stat. Ann. Title 25 Sec. 1402

Oklahoma continued
Accessibility–Publicly owned and funded buildings; BOCA and
   Oklahoma.
   OKLA. Stat. Ann. Title 61 Sec. 11
Contact–Governor's Committee on Employment of the
   Handicapped
   4300 N. Lincoln Boulevard
   Oklahoma City, Oklahoma 73105
   (405) 521-3756 (Voice/TDD)
   (800) 522-8224 (Voice/TDD)
Human Rights Commission
   2101 N. Lincoln Boulevard
   Oklahoma City, Oklahoma 73105
   (405) 521-3441

OREGON

Employment–Physical. Mental. AIDS. (1) OR. Rev. Stat. 659.400
   and 433.045
AIDS–Covered. Policy letter 3/86.
   OR. Rev. Stat. 433.045 (ch. 878, eff. 10/3/89)
   Health Division Rules on AIDS (1988).
   OR. Admin. R. Title 333 Sec. 12.
Public Accommodations–Physical. Mental. OR. Rev. Stat. 659.425
   White Cane Law. OR. Rev. Stat. 346.610
Housing–Physical. Mental. OR. Rev. Stat. 659.430
   White Cane Law. OR. Rev. Stat. 346.630
Education–Physical. Mental. OR. Rev. Stat. 659.150
Accessibility–Public. Private.
   ANSI A117.1-1980 and Oregon.
   OR. Rev. Stat. 447.210 et seq.
Contact–State Commission for the Handicapped
   1880 Lancaster, Suite 106
   Salem, Oregon 97301
   (503) 378-3142 (Voice)
   (503) 378-3599 (TDD)

Oregon continued
Bureau of Labor and Industries
Civil Rights Division,
State Office Building, 2d. Floor
1400 S.W. Fifth Avenue
Portland, Oregon 97201
(503) 229-5900, 229-6601
(800) 452-7813

PENNSYLVANIA

Employment–Physical. Mental. (4) 43 PA. Stat. Ann. 955
("Non-job related handicap/disability")
AIDS–Covered: Policy Memorada 1/86 and 6/88
Public Accommodations–Physical. Mental. 43 PA. Stat. Ann. 955
Housing–Physical. Mental. 43 PA. Stat. Ann. Sec. 955
Education–Within definition of public accommodation. 43 PA.
Stat. Ann. 955
Accessibility–Public. Private.
ANSI A117.1-1980 and Pennsylvania.
71 PA. Stat. Ann. 1455
Contact–Governor's Committee on Employment of People with
Disabilities
Labor and Industry Building
7th and Forster Streets
Harrisburg, Pennsylvania 17120
(717) 787-5244
Human Relations Commission
101 S. Second Street
P.O. Box 3145
Harrisburg, Pennsylvania 17105-3145
(717) 787-4412, 787-4410

RHODE ISLAND

Employment–Physical. Mental. (4) R.I. Gen. Laws 28-5-7
State funded or regulated. R.I. Gen. Laws 42-87-1 et seq.
White Cane Law. R.I. Gen. Laws 40-9-1.
AIDS–Covered. Commission on Human Rights Policy Letter 6/86
Repression and Suppression of Contagious Diseases Act:
Housing, employment, public accommodations. R.I. Gen.
Laws 23-6:10-24.

Rhode Island *continued*

Public Accommodations–White Cane Law. R.I. Gen. Laws 40-9-1
Also see R.I. Gen. Laws 42-87-1 et seq. prohibiting discrimination in any program, activity, or service regulated or funded by the state.

Housing–Physical. Mental. R.I. Gen. Laws 34-37-1
Also see R.I. Gen. Laws 28-5.1-1 and 42-87-1, both et seq.

Education–Physical. Mental. R.I. Gen. Laws. 28-5.1-1 and 42-87-1, both et seq.
White Cane Law. R.I. Gen. Laws 40-9-1

Accessibility–Public. Private.
ANSI-1980 and Rhode Island.
R.I. Gen.Laws 23-27.3 et seq., 37-8-15
Also see R.I. Gen. Laws 42-109-1, general nondiscrimination law (1990).

Contact–Governor's Commission on the Handicapped
Building 51, 3rd Floor
Providence, Rhode Island 02908-5686
(401) 277-3731 (Voice/TDD)

Commission on Human Rights
10 Abbott Park Place
Providence, Rhode Island 02903
(401) 277-2661

SOUTH CAROLINA

Employment–Physical. Mental. (15) S.C. Code Ann. 43-33-530
Also, S.C. Code Ann. 43-33-210 on testing for persons unable to use written or visual material.
White Cane Law S.C. Code Ann. 43-33-60

AIDS–

Public Accommodations–Physical. Mental. S.C. Code Ann. 43-33-530
White Cane Law. S.C. Code Ann. 43-33-20 et seq.

Housing–Physical. Mental. S.C. Code 43-33-530
White Cane Law. S.C. Code Ann. 43-33-70

Education–Physical. Mental. S.C. Code Ann. 43-33-530

Accessibility–Public. Private
Latest ANSI and Southern Building Code S.C. Code 10-5-210 et seq.

South Carolina continued
  Contact–Governor's Committee on Employment of the
    Handicapped
  S.C. Vocational Rehabilitation Department
  1410 Boston Avenue
  Box 15
  West Columbia, South Carolina 29171
  (803) 737-6570, 737-6571
  Human Affairs Commission
  2611 Forest Drive
  P.O. Drawer 4490
  Columbia, South Carolina 29204
  (803) 737-6570, 737-6571

SOUTH DAKOTA
  Employment–Physical. Mental. (1) S.D.C.L.A. 20-13-10
  AIDS–
  Public Accommodations–Physical. Mental. S.D.C.L.A. 20-13-23
    White Cane Law. S.D.C.L.A. 20-13-23.1
  Housing–Physical. Mental. S.D.C.L.A. 20-13-20
  Education–Physical. Mental. S.D.C.L.A. 20-13-22
  Accessibility–Public owned or funded.
    ANSI A117.1-1980 and South Dakota.
    S.D.C.L.A. 5-14-13 et seq
    Also see S.D.C.L.A. 9-46-1-wheelchair curb ramps–most
    current ANSI
  Contact–Division of Human Rights
    State Capitol Building
    500 East Capitol Street
    Pierre, South Dakota 57501-5070
    (605) 773-4493
  Governor's Advisory Committee on Employment of People with
    Disabilities
    Department of Human Services
    700 Governors Drive
    Pierre, South Dakota 57501-2275
    (605) 773-5990

TENNESSEE
  Employment–Physical. Mental. Visual. (8) TENN. Code Ann.
    8-50-103
  AIDS–Employment. Covered within TENN. Code Ann. 8-50-103

Tennessee *continued*
Public Accommodations–No. TENN. Code Ann. 4-21-501
  White Cane Law. TENN. Code Ann. 62-7-112
Housing–No. TENN. Code Ann. 4-21-601
  Physical. TENN. Code Ann. 66-7-104
Education–White Cane Law. TENN. Code Ann. 62-7-112
Accessibility–Public. Private.
  North Carolina Illustrated Handbook.
  TENN. Code Ann. 68-18-201
Contact–Governor's Committee for Disabled Persons
  Division of Rehabilitation Services
  Citizens Plaza Building
  400 Deaderick Street
  Nashville, Tennessee 37219
  (615) 741-2095
Human Rights Commission
  Capitol Boulevard Building
  226 Capitol Boulevard
  Nashville, Tennessee 37219-5095
  (615) 741-5825

TEXAS

Employment–Physical. Mental. Mentally Retarded. (1 in public &
  15 in private employment)
  TEXAS Code Ann. Human Resources 121.003
  TEXAS Civil Stats. Vol. 16a, Title 92 Art. 5521K
  TEXAS Human Rights Comm. Sec. 1.01
AIDS–Communicable Disease Act (1987)
  AIDS Testing, TEXAS Civil Stats. 4419b-1.
  Covered: Attorney General's Opinion 3/87
Public Accommodations–Physical. TEXAS Code Ann. Human
  Resources 121.003
Housing–Physical. TEXAS Code Ann. Human Resources 121.003
Education–Physical (within definition of public facilities).
  TEXAS Code Ann. Human Resources 121.003
Accessibility–Public. Private.
  ANSI A117.1-1980 and TEXAS.
  TEXAS Rev. Stat. Art. 601B, Art. 7 Sec. 7.01

Texas continued
Contact–Governor's Committee for Disabled Persons
4900 North Lamar
Austin, Texas 78751-2316
(512) 483-4381
Commission on Human Rights
Box 13493
Capitol Station
8100 Cameron Station
Austin, Texas 78711
(512) 837-8534

UTAH

Employment–Physical. Mental. (15) UTAH Code Ann. 34-35-1
White Cane Law. UTAH Code Ann. 26-30-3
AIDS–Covered: Opinion of Attorney General 1986, Testing For
Medical Personnel: UTAH Code Ann. 26-6a-1.
Public Accommodations–White Cane Law. UTAH Code Ann.
26-30-1
Housing–White Cane Law. encompasses. UTAH Code Ann.
26-30-1 and 26-30-2.
Education–
Accessibility–Publicly owned or funded.
Utah.
UTAH Code Ann. 26-29-1 et seq. Utah continued
Contact–Governor's Committee on Employment of The
Handicapped.
120 North 200 West
P.O. Box 45500
Salt Lake City, Utah 84145
(801) 538-4210
Industrial Commission
Anti-Discrimination Division
160 East 3rd Street South
Salt Lake City, Utah 84111-0870
(801) 530-6922

VERMONT

Employment–Physical. Mental. (1) 21 VT. Stat. Ann. 494 et seq
AIDS–Fair Employment Practices Act prohibits mandatory AIDS
testing as a condition of employment. 21 VT. Stat. Ann. 494 et
seq.

Vermont continued
Public Accommodations–Physical. Mental.
  9 VT. Stat. Ann. Ch. 139
Housing–Physical. Mental. 9 VT. Stat. Ann. Ch. 139
Education–Physical. Mental. (within definition of public
  accommodations.) 9 VT. Stat. Ann. Ch. 139
Accessibility–Public. Private.
  ANSI A117.1-1980 and Vermont.
  18 VT. Stat. Ann. 1321 et seq.
Contact–Attorney General of Vermont
  Civil Rights Division
  Pavilion Office Building
  109 State Street
  Montpelier, Vermont 05602
  (802) 828-3171
Vermont Human Rights Commission
  National Life Drive
  Montpelier, Vermont 05602
  (802) 828-2480
Governor's Committee on Employment of People with Disabilities
  D.D. Council
  103 South Main Street
  Waterbury, Vermont 05676
  (802) 241-2612

VIRGINIA

Employment–Physical. Mental. (1) VA Code 51.01-41
  VA Code 2.1-716
AIDS–Department of Personnel Guidelines Public Employee
  5/10/88
Public Accommodations–Physical. Mental. VA Code 51.01-44
  VA Code 2.1-715
Housing–Physical. Mental. VA Code 51.01-45
Education–Physical. Mental. VA Code 51.01-42
  VA Code 2.1-715
Accessibility–Public. Private
  ANSI A117.1-1980 and Virginia.
  VA Code 2.1-514 et seq., 15.1-381

Virginia continued
Contact–Department of Rights for the Disabled
James Monroe Building
101 North 14th Street
Richmond, Virginia 23219
(804) 225-2042
1-800-552-3962
Department of Labor and Industry
Box 12064
Richmond, Virginia 23241
(804) 786-2376
Fair Housing Administrator
Department of Commerce
3600 W. Broad Street
Richmond, Virginia 23230
(804) 257-8530

WASHINGTON

Employment–Sensory. Physical. Mental. AIDS. (8)
WASH Rev. Code Ann. 49.60.172, 49.60.174,
WASH Rev. Code Ann. 49.60.180-49.60.200
White Cane Law. Public Employment
WASH.Rev. Code Ann. 70.84.080
AIDS–Covered: Human Rights Commission Policy Guidelines
12/86
Poster 7/86 WASH. Rev. Code Ann. 49.60.172 and 49.60.174
Public Accommodations–Sensory. Physical. Mental.
WASH Rev. Code Ann. 49.60.215
White Cane Law. WASH. Rev. Code Ann. 70.84.010
Housing–Sensory. Physical. Mental. WASH Rev. Code. Ann.
49.60.222-49.227
Education–Within definition of public accommodation. See
WASH. Rev. Code Ann. 49.60.040 and 49.60.215
Accessibility–Public. Private.
ANSI A117.1 and Washington.
RCW 70.92.100

Washington *continued*
Contact–Governor's Committee on Disability
Issues and Employment,
Employment Services Division
Employment Security Building, KG 11
212 Maple Park
Olympia, Washington 98504
(206) 438-3168
Human Rights Commission
402 Evergreen Plaza Building
711 South Capitol Way
Olympia, Washington 98504-3341
(206) 753-2558, 753-6770

WEST VIRGINIA

Employment–Physical. Mental. (12) W.VA Code 5-11-9
White Cane Law W.VA Code 5-15-7
AIDS–Covered: case law.
Testing. W.VA. Code 16-3c-1
Public Accommodations–Physical. Mental. W.VA Code 5-11-9
White Cane Law. W.VA Code 5-15-4
Housing–Physical. Mental. W.VA Code 5-11-9
Education–Physical. Mental. (Within definition public
accommodation) W.VA. Code 5-11-9
Accessibility–Publicly owned or used.
ANSI A117.1-1961/71 and West Virginia.
W.VA. Code 18-10F-1
Contact–Governor's Committee on Disabled Persons
Director, Division of Rehabilitation Services
State Capitol Building
Charlestown, West Virginia 25305
(304) 766-4601
Human Rights Commission
215 Professional Boulevard
1036 Quarrier Street
215 Professional Building
Charlestown, West Virginia 25301
(304) 348-2616

WISCONSIN

Employment–Physical. Mental. (1) WIS. Stat. Ann. 111.321
AIDS–Covered. Case Law. Testing. WIS. Stat. Ann. 103.15
Public Accommodations–Physical. Developmentally Disabled.
WIS. Stat. Ann. 942.04
White Cane Law. WIS. Stat. Ann. 174.056
Housing–Physical. Mental. WIS. Stat. Ann. 101.22
Education–Physical or developmentally disabled in
post-secondary or vocational. WIS. Stat. Ann. 101.223
Accessibility–Public. Private.
Most current ANSI and Wisconsin.
WIS. Stat. Ann. 101.01 and 101.13
Contact–Governor's Committee for People with Disabilities
131 West Wilson
Box 7852
Madison, Wisconsin 53707
(608) 266-5378, 266-9248 (Voice)
(608) 267-2082 (TDD)
Department of Labor, Industry and Human Relations
Wisconsin Equal Rights Division
201 East Washington Avenue
Madison, Wisconsin 53708
(608) 266-6860

WYOMING

Employment–Physical. Mental. (2)WYO. Stat. Ann. 27-9-101
AIDS–
Public Accommodations–No. WYO. Stat. 6-9-101
White Cane Law. WYO. Stat. 42-1-126
Housing–
Education–
Accessibility–Publicly owned or funded.
ANSI A117.1-1961/71 and Wyoming
WYO. Stat. 35-13-101
Contact–Governor's Committee on Employment of The
Handicapped
Herschler Building, Room 1101
Cheyenne, Wyoming 82002
(307) 777-7191 (Voice and TDD)
(307) 777-7385

Wyoming continued
Fair Employment Practices Commission
  Hershler Building
  122 West 25th Street
  Cheyenne, Wyoming 82002
  (307) 777-7261

FEDERAL CONTACTS

The federal system of statutes, regulations, agencies, and programs is, at best, a myriad of mazes. At worst, it can be an unending labyrinth of bureaucracy. There are however, definitive points of entry into the federal establishment at which assistance may be available.

In this appendix, the key executive agencies as well as the key committees and subcommittees of Congress are identified to provide the reader with points of contact with the preeminent institutional entities.

Federal law now prohibits discrimination against qualified persons with disabilities in employment, in the use and enjoyment of places of public accommodations, in housing, in receiving services and particpating in the programs and activities of state and local governments, recipients of federal aid, and the federal government. Federal contractors must take affirmative action in hiring and promoting qualified individuals with disabilities. Accessibility is mandated in new, altered and leased federal and non-federal buildings, though with non-federal leases the emphasis will generally be on a program or activity basis within the structure.

On a day-to-day basis the federal executive agencies may have more practical information than the congressional sources. Accordingly, they are set forth first. The federal agencies are grouped by responsibilities under the Americans with Disabilities Act, Rehabilitation Act, Fair Housing Act, Architectural Barriers Act, and Individuals with Disabilities Education Act. Where to obtain accessibility standards, both the Uniform Federal Accessibility Standard (UFAS) and ANSI, is noted. Also identified are those other federal agencies, which, while not part of the "civil rights" legislative mandate or regulatory framework, do have vital information and/or the ability to direct the inquirer to entities and organizations which can be helpful.

Readers should also keep in mind that many of the larger agencies, such as the Departments of Labor, Health and Human Services, or Education, are not limited in their programs to Washington, D.C. and do have offices in the "federal" regional cities: Boston, New York, Philadelphia, Atlanta, Chicago, Kansas City (MO), Dallas, Denver, San Francisco, and Seattle. Local telephone directories in those cities will contain listings for those agencies under "United States Government." Readers should feel free to consult regional sources as well as those at the headquarters offices noted below.

On the practical side, bear in mind that in interacting with any large organization, persistence in seeking information is a definite necessity. It is also wise to keep track of the name, telephone number, and address of people with whom you speak. Finally, if an official is unable to be of assistance, remember to ask them who can help you.

Executive Agencies

Americans with Disabilities Act (ADA) and Rehabilitation Act

Department of Justice

Civil Rights Division
Office of Coordination and Review
320–1st Street, NW
Washington, D.C. 20530

ADA Information – Coordination and Review Section

P.O. Box 66118
Washington, DC 20035-6118
(202) 307-2222 (Voice or TDD)
(202) 514-0301 (Voice); (202) 514-0381 (TDD)

ADA: State and Local Government Programs and Activities, Public Accommodations, Technical Assistance, Coordination of ADA, Titles II, III, V

Rehabilitation Act: Section 504 Nondiscrimination by Federal Grantees, Coordination of Rehabilitation Act

Equal Employment Opportunity Commission

1800 L Street, NW
Washington, D.C. 20507
(202) 663-4900 (Voice)
1-800-USA-EEOC (Voice)
1-800-800-3302 (TDD)

ADA: Employment, Title I

Rehabilitation Act: Federal Government Employment, Section 501

Architectural Transportation Barriers Compliance Board
1111–18th Street, NW
5th Floor
Washington, D.C. 20036
(202) 653-7834 (voice or TDD)
(800) 663-3372 (voice or TDD)

ADA: Minimum Guidelines and Requirements for Accessible Design, Titles II and III

Rehabilitation Act: Accessibility Enforcement, Guidelines and Technical Assistance, Section 502

Department of Transportation
Assistant General Counsel for Regulation and Enforcement
400–7th Street, SW
Washington, D.C. 20590
(202) 366-4723 (voice)
(202) 755-7687 (TDD)

Urban Mass Transportation Administration
400–7th Street, SW
Washington, D.C. 20590
(202) 366-4040

ADA: Bus and rail vehicles and services, Titles II and III

Rehabilitation Act: Programs/activities, Section 504

Americans with Disabilities Act

Federal Communications Commission
Common Carriers Bureau
1919 M Street, NW
Washington, D.C. 20554
(202) 632-6910, 632-7000 (voice); (202) 632-6999 (TDD)
Telecommunications, Title IV

Rehabilitation Act

Department of Labor, Office of Federal Contract Compliance Programs

200 Constitution Avenue, NW
Washington, D.C. 20210
(202) 523-9475

Affirmative action by federal contractors, Section 503

Fair Housing Act and Rehabilitation Act

Department of Housing and Urban Development

Office of HUD Program Compliance-Fair Housing
451–7th Street, SW
Washington, D.C. 20410
(202) 708-0836, 708-2616, 619-8041
(800) 424-8590 (voice), (800) 543-8294 (TDD)

Fair Housing Act: General non-discrimination in housing
Rehabilitation Act: Programs/activities, Section 504

Architectural Barriers Act

Accessibility in Buildings and Uniform Federal Accessibility Standard

General Services Administration

Public Buildings Service
18th & F Streets, NW
Washington, D.C. 20405
(202) 501-0971

Department of Defense

Office of Assistant Secretary (Equal Opportunity)
The Pentagon, Room 3E317
Washington, D.C. 20301
(202) 697-8661

Department of Housing and Urban Development
Office of Intergovernmental Relations
451–7th Street, SW, Room 10140
Washington, D.C. 20410
(202) 708-0030, 708-0720

United States Postal Service
Real Estate and Buildings Department
475 L'Enfant Plaza West, SW
Washington, D.C. 20260–6424
(202) 268-3139

NOTE: The ANSI A117.1 standard is available from:

American National Standard Institute
1430 Broadway
New York, New York 10018
(212) 642-4900

Indivuduals with Disabilities Education Act
(formerly EAHCA)

Department of Education
Assistant Secretary for Special Education and Rehabilitation
    Services
330 C Street, SW
Washington, D.C. 20202
(202) 732-1265

Department of Education
Office of Special Education Programs
330 C Streets, SW
Washington, D.C. 20202
(202) 732-1007

Other Federal Agencies

National Council on Disability

800 Independence Avenue, SW, Room 814
Washington, D.C. 20591
(202) 267-3235
(202) 267-3232 (TDD)

President's Committee on Employment of People with Disabilities

1111–20th Street, NW, Room 636
Washington, D.C. 20036
(202) 653-5044
Job Accomodations Network: (800) JAN-7234 (voice/TDD–
  U.S. outside West Virginia.)
(800) JAN-INWV (voice/TDD-West Virginia)
(800) JAN-CANA (voice/TDD-Canada)

Rehabilitation Services Administration

330 C Street, SW, Room 3024
Washington, D.C. 20202
(202) 732-1282

National Institutes of Mental Health

5600 Fishers Lane; Room 1799
Rockville, Maryland 20852
(301) 443-3673

Social Security Administration, Office of Disability

Altmeyer Building, 6401 Security Building
Baltimore, Maryland 21235
(301) 965-3424
(800) 234-5772

Administration on Developmental Disabilities

Hubert Humphrey Building, Room 329D
200 Independence Avenue, SW
Washington, D.C. 20201
(202) 245-2890 (voice/TDD)

National Information Center for Children & Youth with Handicaps (NICHY)

7926 Jones Branch Drive, Suite 1100
McLean, VA 22102
(703) 893-6061
(800) 999-5599

President's Committee on Mental Retardation

Wilbur J. Cohen Federal Building, Room 4723
330 Independence Avenue, SW
Washington, D.C. 20201
(202) 619-0634

Congress

United States Senate

Labor and Human Resources Committee
SD-428, Dirksen Senate Office Building
Washington, D.C. 20510
(202) 224-5375 (Voice)
(202) 224-3457 (TDD)

Subcommittee on Disability Policy
SH-113, Hart Senate Office Building
Washington, D.C. 20510
(202) 224-6265 (Voice)
(202) 224-3457 (TDD)

Environment and Public Works Committee
Subcommittee on Water Resources, Transportation and
  Infrastructure
SD-460, Dirksen Senate Office Building
Washington, D.C. 20510
(202) 224-3596, 224-6176

Committee on Appropriations
SD-131, Dirksen Senate Office Building
Washington, D.C. 20510
(202) 224-3471

**Subcommittee on Labor, Health and Human Services,
Education and Related Agencies**
SD-180, Dirksen Senate Office Building
Washington, D.C. 20510
(202) 224-7290

United States House of Representatives

Education and Labor Committee
2181 Rayburn
Washington, D.C. 20515
(202) 225-4527

Subcommittee on Select Education
617 House Office Building Annex 1
Washington, D.C. 20515
(202) 226-7532

Public Works and Transportation Committee
Subcommittee on Public Buildings and Grounds
2165 Rayburn
Washington, D.C. 20515
(202) 225-4472, 225-9961

Appropriations Committee
Capitol Building, Room H-218
Washington, D.C. 20515
(202) 225-2771

Subcommittee on Labor, Health and Human Services, Education and Related Agencies
2358 Rayburn
Washington, D.C. 20515
(202) 225-3508

Assistance and Information on the Congress

(202) 224-3121

AIDS

The subject of communicable diseases, particularly AIDS (Acquired Immune Deficiency Syndrome), has continued to be important. AIDS in now generally recognized as a disability under the Americans with Disability Act, Rehabilitation Act, and many state and local laws. There are issues of the health and rights of individuals infected with the AIDS virus, individuals who are HIV positive carriers, and the general public. Public and private sector policies and practices related to persons with AIDS are evolving.

Reprinted are examples of policies, employment practices, and contract provisions relating to individuals with communicable diseases, such as AIDS. The most effective solutions are developed from the cooperative efforts of business/government/unions/concerned entities. Readers are reminded that the Americans with Disabilities Act does not supersede state/local laws which provide equal or greater protection for individuals with disabilities, including persons with AIDS.

The state and federal agencies, and congressional contacts, in the first two appendices may have information. Here are some additional sources of information, technical and legal, on this most dynamic of issues.

FAIRFAX COUNTY, VIRGINIA, SCHOOL BOARD
Policies, Practices, and Provisions
Adopted May 12, 1988.
Revised July 26, 1990

Policy 4265.1
School Board

PERSONNEL SERVICES
Employment Actions
Human Immunodeficiency Virus (HIV)

I. PURPOSE

To establish policy regarding employees who are infected with the Human Immunodeficiency Virus (HIV).

II. PHILOSOPHY

The School Board recognizes its dual obligation to protect the rights of individual employees infected with HIV and to provide a safe environment for students, staff, and the public. According to current medical knowledge and guidelines issued by the U.S. Centers for Disease Control, there is insignificant risk of transmission of HIV within the workplace/school setting. Employees who have HIV or an HIV-related condition shall be permitted to continue in their present assignment as long as they are medically able to do so, are performing their jobs satisfactorily, and medical evidence indicates that their condition poses no unreasonable risk to themselves or to others.

III. PROCEDURES

A. Assessment of Medical Condition

As with other medical conditions, employees who are infected with HIV need not routinely inform school officials unless (1) their physicians advise them that a significant health problem will prevent them from doing their job, (2) their illness requires special accommodation from their employer, or (3) they may transmit a disease to others.

An employee with an HIV-related condition may be asked to provide medical information from the employee's physician and/or submit to an examination by the school system's physician in the following circumstances:

a. if the employee has requested accommodation, such as modification of the employee's position or reassignment to another position, because of the employee's HIV -related condition, or

b. if the employee's medical condition appears to be affecting that employee's job performance adversely, or

c. if the employee's condition constitutes a direct threat to the health or safety of others.

B. Job Assignments

An employee diagnosed with AIDS or an HIV-related condition may request modification of his or her assignment, reassignment to another position, or other reasonable accommodation. Such requests shall be submitted in writing to the assistant superintendent for the Department of Personnel Services or designee, who shall decide what medical information is needed, and determine the employee's assignment.

IV. **RIGHTS OF EMPLOYEES**

At any time during this process an employee may be accompanied by or represented by a person of the employee's choosing.

The right of the employee to privacy shall be respected by all persons involved in the implementation and monitoring of this policy. These persons shall maintain confidentiality in compliance with policy, regulations, and state law.

The number of personnel advised of the employee's medical condition shall be kept at the minimum needed to ensure policy implementation and to ensure that the safety and health of other individuals are not directly threatened. The assistant superintendent for the Department of Personnel Services, or designee, shall determine who needs to know an employee's medical condition on a case-by-case basis, and shall maintain confidential records of who is informed and when.

Information pertaining to an employee's condition shall be conveyed to those who need to know on an individual basis by direct, in person, verbal communication. The employee shall be informed of whom the administration informs of his or her condition.

Any and all records pertaining to the medical condition of an employee with HIV or who has an HIV-related condition shall be placed in a sealed file with concurrence of the employee. The assistant superintendent for the Department of Personnel Services shall maintain and with the employee, or designee, shall have access to the sealed file.

Any employee who disagrees with the decision of the assistant superintendent for the Department of Personnel Services, or designee, shall be entitled to appeal the decision according to existing procedures.

V. BENEFITS

Employees who are disabled by HIV or an HIV-related condition shall be entitled to the same benefits as other employees temporarily or permanently disabled by illness including, but not limited to, sick leave, sick leave bank, and disability retirement. The benefits available in any particular case will be determined in accordance with the terms then in effect of the benefit policy or plan under which benefits are sought, as interpreted in the discretion of the administrator of that plan or policy. Benefit plans and policies available to FCPS employees are subject to change from time to time at the School Board's discretion.

VI. EDUCATION AND SUPPORT

The Superintendent shall implement a program of ongoing education relative to HIV for all employees, including full-time, part-time, and temporary professional and support staff, to ensure that all employees are informed, in a consistent manner, about:

- The nature of HIV infection, including how it is and is not transmitted according to current medical research;
- FCPS procedures related to employees and students with AIDS and HIV infection;
- Resources within the school division and community for obtaining additional information or assistance; and
- Preventative hygiene procedures to avoid the spread of infectious diseases.

For non-English-speaking employees, this education shall be provided in their primary language, if feasible.

In addition, appropriate, job-related training shall be provided to specific employee groups. New personnel shall be provided with education relative to AIDS before beginning work.

Development and provision of this education program shall be coordinated with the Fairfax County Department of Health.

VII. MEDICAL ADVISORY COMMITTEE

The Superintendent shall appoint a committee to advise him regarding changes in the state of HIV-related medical knowledge based on documented medical research that may result in revisions to this policy. The committee shall be comprised primarily of medical professionals with expertise relative to HIV. It shall rely primarily on the U.S. Public Health Service and the State Department of Health for documentation of new information relative to HIV.

See also: Policy 4220, Personnel Files; Regulation 4220, Personnel Files; Policy 4460, Grievance Procedures; Regulation 4461, Grievance Procedure—Teachers and Instructional Aides; Regulation 4462, Grievance Procedure—Civil Service Employees; Regulation 4463, Grievance Procedure—Food Service Employees; Regulation 4464, Grievance Procedure—Bus Drivers and Aides; Regulation 4465, Grievance Procedures—Educational Administrative and Supervisory Employees; Policy 4790, Sick Leave Banks Regulation 4790.1, Sick Leave

Legal reference: Code of Virginia, Sections: 22.1-272, Contagious and Infectious Diseases Policy

Fairfax County Public Schools

Notice 2108
Student Services
and Special Education
—Latt
August 27, 1990

STUDENT SERVICES
Health and Welfare
Human Immunodeficiency Virus (HIV)

This notice will be effective until September 30, 1991.

I. PURPOSE
  To delineate the use of the form, "Release of Information for Medical Conditions."

II. USE
  The form, "Release of Information for Medical Conditions," is to be initiated by the first Fairfax County Public Schools staff member informed by a parent, guardian, or adult student of a student's HIV condition. The staff member is to secure written consent to share knowledge of the student's diagnosed HIV condition for himself or herself, the deputy superintendent for school operations, the assistant superintendent for the Department of Student Services and Special Education, the principal of the student's school, the health liaison official with the Department of Student Services and Special Education, the school public health nurse, the clinic room aide, the guidance director, the student's teacher(s) , and other staff that the parent, guardian, or adult student deem appropriate.

Attachment
SLD-1

Attachment
Notice 2108
August 27, 1990

CONFIDENTIAL

CONFIDENTIAL

Fairfax County Public Schools Fairfax, Virginia
Release Of Information for Medical Conditions

Student Name _____

	Last	First	Middle

Date of Birth _____ Grade ____ Sex _____

School _____ Student ID _____

I hereby permit Fairfax County Public Schools to inform the persons and/or agencies indicated below of _____ (medical condition) for the student named above.

Person or Agency	Title or Position	Parent Initial
_____	Deputy Superintendent School Operations	_____
_____	Assistant Superintendent Department of Student Services and Special Education	
_____	Principal	_____
_____	Health Liaison Department of Student Services and Special Education	_____
_____	Public Health Nurse	_____
_____	Clinic Room Aide	_____
_____	Guidance Director and/or Counselor	_____
_____	Teacher	_____
_____	Teacher	_____

I understand that no one else will have access to this knowledge of medical condition without my expressed written consent except in a life-threatening situation related to the above-named student. In a life-threatening situation, the student information will be restricted to only those professionals assisting the named student.

_____   _____

Signature of Parent, Guardian, or   Date
Student (if 18 years or age or older)

FAIRFAX COUNTY, VIRGINIA, SCHOOL BOARD
Policy
Adopted May 12, 1988
Revised April 5, 1990
Revised July 26, 1990

Policy 2108.2
School Board

STUDENT SERVICES
Health and Welfare
Human Immunodeficiency Virus (HIV)
This policy supersedes Policy 2108.1.

I. **PURPOSE**

To establish policy regarding students who are infected with the Human Immunodeficiency Virus (HIV).

II. **PHILOSOPHY**

The School Board recognizes its dual obligation to protect the rights of individual students infected with HIV and to provide a safe environment for students, staff, and the public. Since it is known that HIV is not transmitted through casual contact, any student who is HIV infected will continue education in a regular classroom assignment unless the health status requires otherwise. Students infected with HIV or who have HIV-related conditions may be excluded from school until it is determined that students' attendance at school does not pose an unreasonable risk to the health and welfare of themselves or others. The School Board shall provide educational setting deemed appropriated. It is the intent of the School Board to follow the recommendations of the U.S. Centers for Disease Control and the Virginia Department of Health that most HIV-infected children be allowed to attend school in an unrestricted setting and that decisions regarding school attendance be based on the medical condition of each child and the expected type of interaction with others in that setting.

III. **PROCEDURES**

A. Identification and Preliminary Review

   1 An adult student or the parent(s) or guardian(s) of a Fairfax County Public Schools student who has a medical diagnosis by a physician as having an HIV-related condition is expected to notify the principal that such a condition exists.

   2. A principal who has reason to believe that a student is infected with HIV shall immediately consult with the assis-

tant superintendent for student services and special education, who will then notify the Fairfax County Health Department. The assistant superintendent for the student services and special education or designee will consult with the individual's family and physician, when appropriate, and the Fairfax County Health Department to determine whether the student is well enough to stay in school. Unless the health status of the student interferes significantly with the student's current classroom assignment, every effort will be made to support the student's regular attendance in school. The Fairfax County Health Department will make a recommendation based on a medical record or finding whether the student shall be temporarily excluded from school attendance pending review. If recommended, the principal shall temporarily exclude that student from daily school attendance.

3. Temporary exclusion or temporary inclusion shall continue until all pertinent information is obtained, a comprehensive review process is completed, and the Superintendent has acted.

4. The principal shall:

    ● confer with the adult student or the student's parent(s) or guardian(s) prior to temporarily excluding or including the student;

    ● provide the adult student or the parent(s) or guardian(s) with a copy of this policy;

    ● notify the adult student or the parent(s) or guardian(s), orally and in writing in their primary language, if feasible, of the temporary exclusion or review procedure of the student who is not excluded; and

    ● ensure that appropriate instructional activities will be provided to the student during the period of temporary exclusion.

5. The Superintendent shall:

    ● inform the School Board regarding the temporary exclusion of the student;

    ● ensure that school personnel cooperate with public health personnel in completing and coordinating immunization data, exemptions, and exclusions, and collaborate with public and private organizations in the provision of support services to HIV-infected students as required by the Model Guidelines for School Attendance for Children with HIV; and

● ensure that all individuals will be informed of the situation on a "Need to Know" basis with written consent of the parent(s), guardian(s), or adult student.

B. Panel Review

1. The Superintendent shall establish a Review Committee following adoption of this policy by the School Board. Review panels drawn from the committee established by the Superintendent shall include a representative of the Fairfax County Health Department, designated by the Director of Health; a representative of the Fairfax County Public Schools, designated by the Superintendent, who will serve as a chairperson; a mental health professional; an independent medical expert; and others deemed appropriate to the review. The assistant superintendent for student services and special education shall convene the review panel after gathering all pertinent information necessary to determine the appropriate status of the student, including medical records provided by the student's family and physician.

2. The student, the student's parent(s) or guardian(s), the student's physician, the student's attorney, and the principal or a representative of the child's school may attend the review and provide information shared with the panel shall be confidential.

3. The review panel shall evaluate the HIV-infected student's condition and make recommendations regarding an appropriate educational setting and instructional program.

4. The degree of risk to the student and to others with whom the student may come into contact shall be the prime consideration. The review panel may require that additional medical and other appropriate information be obtained prior to completion of the review process. Each case shall be handled on its own merits, with due consideration of the student's medical condition, and expected type of interaction with others.

   The review panel shall provide all information and findings, including consideration of an appropriate instructional program and educational setting for the student, to the Director of the Fairfax County Health Department. The Director of the Fairfax County Health Department shall be asked to make a recommendation to the Superintendent regarding the student's attendance in school, an appropriate educational setting, the schedule for periodic reexamination of the student's condition, and further recommendations as deemed appropriate. If a change in the student's program is necessary, the Superintendent or designee, family, and physician or health department official will develop an individual plan which is medically, legally, and educationally sound. If the HIV-infected student is receiving special services, the services will be in agreement with established policies.

The adult student or the parent(s) or guardian(s) shall be notified in writing of the Superintendent's decision within five working days of the receipt of the Director of the Health Department's recommendation. The process from original notification to the adult student or the parent(s) or guardian(s) to the final decision of the Superintendent shall not exceed a total of 30 days. A time extension may be granted if adequate information is not available for consideration or for other good cause.

The Superintendent's decision shall include provision for:

● information regarding the availability of counseling for the student and the student's family;

● monitoring of the student's condition;

● reconsideration upon receipt of new information at a later date;

● further collaboration with public and private organizations in the provision of support services to HIV-infected students.

IV. RIGHTS OF STUDENT(S)/PARENT(S) AND COMPLIANCE WITH CONFIDENTIALITY

Persons involved in the implementation and monitoring of this policy shall maintain confidentiality of records in compliance with state law, School Board policy and regulation. The number of personnel aware of the student's medical condition shall be kept at the minimum needed to ensure implementation of this policy and to ensure appropriate educational and health services are provided to the student. All persons privileged with any medical information about HIV-infected students shall be required to treat all proceedings, discussions, and documents as confidential information.

An adult student or a parent or guardian of the HIV-infected student or the student's attorney may appeal the Superintendent's decision to the School Board by filing with the Clerk of the School Board the written reasons why such decision should be reversed. The School Board shall consider the appeal, if possible, within ten working days and may provide for presentations by the Superintendent or his representatives and the representatives of the student.

V. INSTRUCTION AND SUPPORT

The Superintendent shall implement a program of ongoing information relative to HIV for school staff and all families with children in the Fairfax County Public Schools so that they are informed in a consistent manner about:

- the nature of HIV infection, including how it is and is not transmitted according to current medical research;
- FCPS procedures related to employees and students with an HIV infection or AIDS;
- resources within the school division and community for obtaining additional information or assistance;
- preventative hygiene procedures to avoid the spread of infectious diseases including universal precautions for handling blood and all body fluids within the school setting and on buses.

For non-English-speaking families, this information shall be provided in their primary languages, if feasible.

Development and provision of this information program shall be coordinated with the Fairfax County Health Department.

VI. MEDICAL ADVISORY COMMITTEE

The Superintendent shall appoint a committee to advise him regarding changes in the state of HIV-related medical knowledge based on documented medical research that may result in revisions to this policy. The committee shall be comprised primarily of medical professionals with expertise relative to HIV. It shall rely primarily on the U.S. Public Health Service and the State Department of Health for documentation of new information relative to HIV.

See also: Policy 1450.1, Nondiscrimination—Students; Regulation 1450, Declaration of Nondiscrimination—Handicapped Persons; Policy 4415, Hygiene Practices; Regulation 4415, Hygiene Practices; Policy 2601, Responsibilities and Rights of Students; Regulation 2601.3P, Student Responsibilities and Rights Handbook; Policy 2701, Student Personal Data; Regulation 2701.2, Student Personal Data

Legal reference: Code of Virginia Section: 22.1-271.3, Guidelines for school attendance for children infected with human immunodeficiency virus.

I. Levi Struass & Co. AIDS-related Personnel Policies
   - The company does not have a special, AIDS policy. Instead, it addresses the needs of employees with AIDS and their co-workers within the framework of its general approach to employee relations.
   - The company does not test job applicants for AIDS and there are no AIDS screening questions employment applications.
   - Employees with AIDS/ARC are treated with compassion and understanding—as are employees with any other life threatening disease.
   - Employees with AIDS can continue to work as long as they are medically cleared to do so; they are also eligible for work accommodation.
   - Employees are assured of confidentiality when seeking counseling or medical referral.
   - Company medical coverage, disability leave policy and life insurance do not distinguish between AIDS and any other life threatening disease.
   - The company's medical plan supports home health and hospice care for the terminally ill.
   - A case management strategy is implemented whenever an individual employee becomes critically ill.
   - Managers are held accountable for creating a work environment that is supportive of an employee with AIDS.
   - The company regards itself as having a responsibility to educate its employees so that neither unwarranted fear not prejudice affect the work environment of people with AIDS.
   - Individual, family or group counseling is available to employees and their families through the company's Employee Assistance Program (EAP) or through outside agencies.

- The EAP staff also conducts department and management counseling sessions upon request about issues such as how to handle rumors about AIDS, how to deal directly with people's feelings when a colleague becomes ill with AIDS, what colleagues can do to be helpful to a person with AIDS and how to deal with the grief associated with the death of a colleague.

REPRINTED WITH PERMISSION OF LEVI STRAUSS & CO., SAN FRANCISCO, CA.

COMMUNICABLE DISEASES

Upon written request, an employee shall be provided with information on all communicable diseases to which he/she may have routine workplace exposure. Information provided to employees shall include the symptoms of the diseases, modes of transmission, methods of self-protection, proper workplace procedures, special precautions and recommendations for immunization where appropriate. THE COMMUNICABLE DISEASE POLICY AND ANY SUBSEQUENT REVISIONS WILL BE DISSEMINATED TO THE AGENCY HEALTH AND SAFETY COMMITTEE(S).

The employer recognizes that some employees who work with individuals infected with hepatitis B virus may be at increased risk of acquiring hepatitis B infection. Those employees in an identified "at risk" category, as established by the Center for Disease Control standards, WILL HAVE THE RIGHT TO be vaccinated. Such vaccinations shall be made available at no cost to the employee, for those "at risk" employees who desire it. The Agencies shall identify, with the aid of the Agency Health and Safety Committee(s), those positions and procedures for administering the vaccination program.

If a resident or inmate is found to carry communicable disease, all appropriate precautions shall be taken.
July 1, 1990–December 31, 1991 Section 11.04

Ohio Civil Service Employees Association (OCSEA) Local 11

REPRINTED WITH PERMISSION OF THE AMERICAN FEDERATION OF STATE, COUNTY AND MUNICIPAL EMPLOYEES (AFSCME) UNION.

Federal Executive Agencies

Department of Health and Human Services
Assistant Secretary of Health, National AIDS Program Office
729H Humphrey Building
Washington, D.C.20201
(202) 245-0471

Office of the Surgeon General
716G Humphrey Building
Washington, D.C. 20201
(202) 245-6467

Center For Disease Control
Center for Infectious Diseases
1600 Clifton Road, NE
Atlanta, Georgia 30333
(404) 636-3291 or
(800) 342-2437, 342-AIDS, or
(800) 344-7432 (Hispanic)
(800) 243-7889 (TTY/TDD)

United Stated Department of Labor
Occupational Safety and Health Administration
Health Standards Office
200 Constitution Avenue, NW
Washington, D.C. 20210
(202) 523-7157, 523-7075, 523-8036

Congress

United States Senate

Labor and Human Resources Committee
Health Staff
527 Hart Building
Washington, D.C. 20510
(202) 224-7675

United States House of Representatives

Committee on Energy and Commerce
Subcommittee on Health and the Environment
2415 Rayburn Building
Washington, D.C. 20515
(202) 225-4952

Private Sector

American Management Association
135 West 50th Street
New York, New York 10020
(212) 586-8100

International Personnel Management Association
1617 Duke Street
Alexandria, Virginia 22314
(703) 549-7100

National Gay Rights Advocacy
540 Castro Street
San Francisco, California 94114
(415) 863-3624

American Medical Association
1101 Vermont Avenue, NW
Washington, D.C. 20005
(202) 789-7400

National AIDS Information Clearinghouse
P.O. Box 6003
Rockville, MD 20850
(800) 458-5231, (800) 243-7012 (TTY/TDD)

National Leadership Coalition on AIDS
1150–17th Street, NW
Washington, D.C. 20036
(202) 429-0930

National AIDS Bereavement Center
4300 Old Dominion Drive
Arlington, VA 22207
(703) 522-9758

Human Rights Campaign Fund

1012–14th Street, N.W.
Washington, D.C. 20005
(202) 628-4160

Society for Human Resource Management

606 N. Washington Street
Alexandria, Virginia 22314
(703) 548-3440

State AIDS Programs

ALABAMA

Alabama Department of Public Health
Division of Disease Control
AIDS Prevention Network
State Office Building, Room 756
434 Monroe Street
Montgomery, Alabama 36130-1701
(205) 242-5838, 471-7797

ALASKA

Alaska Department of Health and Social Services
Division of Public Health
Office of Epidemiology
Alaska AIDS Program
3601 C Street, Suite 540
Anchorage, Alaska 99524-0249
(907) 561-4406

ARIZONA

Arizona Department of Health Services
Division of Disease Prevention
AIDS Section
3008 N. 3rd Street, Room 203
Phoenix, Arizona 85012
(602) 230-5819, 255-1292
(800) 334-1540 Hotline

ARKANSAS

Arkansas Department of Health
Sexually Transmitted Diseases Division
AIDS Prevention Program
4815 W. Markham, Room 455
Little Rock, Arkansas 72205-3867
(501) 661-2135

CALIFORNIA
California Department of Health Services
Office Of AIDS
830 S Street
Sacramento, California 94234
(916) 445-0553

COLORADO
Colorado Department of Health
Sexually Transmitted Diseases/AIDS Control
4210 E. 11th Avenue
Denver, Colorado 80220
(303) 331-8320

CONNECTICUT
Connecticut Department of Health Services
AIDS Program
150 Washington Street
Hartford, Connecticut 06106
(203) 566-2048

DELAWARE
Delaware Department of Health and Social Services
Division of Public Health
Bureau of Disease Control
AIDS Program Office
3000 Newport Gap Pike
Building G
Wilmington, Delaware 19808
(302)995-8422

DISTRICT OF COLUMBIA
District of Columbia Department of Human Services
Commission of Public Health
Office of AIDS Administration
1660 L Street NW
Washington, D.C. 20036
(202) 673-6888, 673-3676

FLORIDA
Florida Department of Health and Rehabilitative Services
AIDS Program
1317 Winewood Blvd., Building 6
Tallahassee, Florida 32399-0700
(964) 487-2478

GEORGIA
Georgia Department of Human Resources
Division of Public Health
Offices of Infectious Disease
AIDS Project
878 Peachtree Street, NE
Room 102
Atlanta, Georgia 30309
(404) 894-5304, 894-6428

HAWAII
Hawaii Department of Health
Communicable Disease Division
AIDS and Sexually Transmitted Disease
3627 Kilauea Avenue, Suite 304
Honolulu, Hawaii 96816
(808) 735-5303

IDAHO
Idaho Department of Health and Welfare
Division of Health
Bureau of Preventive Medicine
AIDS Program
450 W. State Street, 4th Fl.
Boise, Idaho 83720
(208) 334-5930

ILLINOIS

Illinois Department of Public Health
Division of Infectious Diseases, AIDS Activity Section
111 N. Canal Street, Room 135
Chicago, Illinois 60601
(312) 814-4846

INDIANA

Indiana Board of Health
Division of Acquired Diseases
Bureau of Disease Intervention
STD and AIDS Section
1330 W. Michigan Street
Indianapolis, Indiana 46206
(317) 633-0851

IOWA

Iowa Department of Public Health
AIDS Prevention Program
Lucas State Office Building
321 E. 12th Street
Des Moines, Iowa 50319-0075
(515) 281-3209
(800) 445-2437–Iowa AIDS Hotline

KANSAS

Kansas Department of Health and Environment Services
Bureau of Disease Control
AIDS Section
Mills Building, Suite 605
109 SW. 9th
Topeka, Kanasa 66612-1271
(913) 296-0022, 296-5588
(800) 232-0040

KENTUCKY
Kentucky Department of Health Services
Communicable Disease Branch
AIDS Program
275 E. Main Street
2nd Floor, E.
Frankfort, Kentucky 40621
(502) 564-4804

LOUISIANA
Louisiana Department of Health and Hospitals
Office of Public Health
AIDS Prevention and Surveillance Project
325 Loyola Avenue Room 618
New Orleans, Louisiana 70160
(504) 568-5508

MAINE
Maine Department of Human Services
Division of Communicable Disease Control
AIDS Prevention Grant Project
State House Station
157 Capitol Street
Augusta, Maine 04333
(207) 289-3747

MARYLAND
Maryland Department of Health and Mental Hygiene
Center for AIDS Related Educational Services
201 W. Preston Street
Baltimore, Maryland 21201
(301) 225-6707

MASSACHUSETTS

Massachusetts Department of Public Health
Division of Commonwealth Disease Control
AIDS Program
305 South Street
Jamaica Plain, Massachusetts 02130
(617) 522-3700

MICHIGAN

Michigan Department of Public Health
Center for Health Promotion
Special Office on AIDS Prevention
3423 N. Logan Street
Lanising, Michigan 48909
(517) 335-8371

MINNESOTA

Minnesota Department of Health
Division of Disease Prevention and Health Promotion
AIDS/STD Prevention Services Section
717 Delaware Street, SE.
Minneapolis, Minnesota 55440
(612) 623-5698

MISSISSIPPI

Mississippi Department of Public Health
AIDS/HIV Prevention Program
2423 N. State Street
Jackson, Mississippi 39215-1700
(601) 960-7723

MISSOURI

Missouri Department of Health
Bureau of AIDS Prevention
1730 E. Elm
Jefferson City, Missouri 65102
(314) 751-6438, 751-6149

MONTANA

Montana Department of Health and Environmental Sciences
AIDS/STD Program
1400 Broadway
Cogswell Building
Helena, Montana 59620
(406)444-4740

NEBRASKA

Nebraska Department of Health
AIDS Program
P.O. Box 95007
Lincoln, Nebraska 68509-5007
(402) 471-4091

NEVADA

Nevada Department of Human Resources
Health Program Division
Communicable Disease Program
505 E. King Street, Room 200
Carson City, Nevada 89710
(702) 885-4800

NEW HAMPSHIRE

New Hampshire Department of Health and Human Services
Division of Public Health Services
Bureau of Disease Control, AIDS Program
6 Hazen Dr.
Health and Human Services Building
Concord, New Hampshire 03301
(603) 271-4477

NEW JERSEY

New Jersey Department of Health
Division of AIDS Prevention and Control
CN 360
363 W. State Street
Trenton, New Jersey 08625-0363
(609) 984-6000

NEW MEXICO

New Mexico Health and Environment Department
AIDS Prevention Program
1190 Street Francis Drive
Santa Fe, New Mexico 87503
(505) 827-0086

NEW YORK

New York Department of Health, Office of Public Health
AIDS Institute
Corning Tower, #503
1315 Empire State Plaza
Albany, New York 12237
(518) 473-7238

NORTH CAROLINA

North Carolina Dept. of Environmental
Health and Natural Resources
Communicable Disease Control Section
AIDS Control Branch
P.O. Box 27687
Raleigh, North Carolina 27611-7687
(919) 733-7301

NORTH DAKOTA

North Dakota Department of Health
Division of Disease Control, AIDS Program
600 East Boulevard
Bismarck, North Dakota 58505-0200
(701) 224-2378

OHIO

Ohio Department of Health
AIDS Unit
246 N. High Street
Columbus, Ohio 43266-0118
(614) 466-5480

OKLAHOMA
Oklahoma Department of Health
AIDS Division
1000 NE. 10th
Oklahoma City, Oklahoma 73105
(405) 271- 4636
(800) 522-9054 (TTY/TDD)
(800) 522-9054–State AIDS Info Line

OREGON
Oregon Department of Human Resources
Health Division
HIV Program
1400 SW. 5th Avenue
Portland, Oregon 97201
(503) 229-5792

PENNSYLVANIA
Pennsylvania Department of Health
AIDS Program
P.O. Box 90, Room 813
Harrisburg, Pennsylvania 17108
(717) 783-0574

RHODE ISLAND
Rhode Island Department of Health
AIDS Program
75 Davis Street
Providence, Rhode Island 02908
(401) 277-2362

SOUTH CAROLINA
South Carolina Dept. of Health and Environmental Control
Bureau of Preventive Health Services
HIV/AIDS Division
AIDS Prevention Program
2600 Bull Street
Columbia, South Carolina 29201
(803) 737-4110

SOUTH DAKOTA

South Dakota Department of Health
Communicable Disease Program
AIDS Prevention and Surveillance Project
523 E. Capitol
Pierre, South Dakota 57501
(605) 773-3364

TENNESSEE

Tennessee Department of Health and Environment
AIDS Program
C2-221 Cordell Hull Building
Nashville, Tennessee 37219
(615) 741-7500

TEXAS

Texas Department of Health
Bureau of Sexually Transmitted Disease Control
HIV Division
1100 W. 49th Street
Austin, Texas 78756
(512) 458-7207

UTAH

Utah Department of Health
Division of Community Health Services
Bureau of Epidemiology
AIDS Control Section
288 N. 1460 W.
Salt Lake City, Utah 84116-0660
(801) 538-6191

VERMONT

Vermont Department of Health
Division of Epidemology
AIDS Program
60 Main Street
Burlington, Vermont 05402
(802) 863-7200

VIRGINIA

Virginia Department of Health
Division of Communicable Disease Control
Sexually Transmitted Disease/AIDS Control Program
109 Governor Street
Richmond, Virginia 23219
(804) 786-6267
(800) 533-4148 (TTY/TDD)

WASHINGTON

Washington Department of Health
Office on HIV/AIDS and Infectious Diseases
Thruston Industrial Park
Building 9, (MS LJ-17)
Olympia, Washington 98504
(206) 586-0426

WEST VIRGINIA

West Virginia Department of Health
Office of Epidemilogy and Health Promotion
Division of Surveillance and Disease Control
AIDS Prevention Program
Building 3, 1900 Kanawha Blvd. E.
Charleston, West Virginia 25305
(304) 348-2950

WISCONSIN

Wisconsin Department of Health and Social Services
Division of Health
1 W. Wilson Street
Madison, Wisconsin 53701-0309
(608) 266-9853

WYOMING

Wyoming Department of Health and Social Services
Division of Health and Medical Services
Preventive Medicine Services
AIDS Prevention Program
Hathaway Building, 4th Floor
Cheyenne, Wyoming 82002-0710
(307) 777-5932
(800) 327-3577 Hotline

Appendix IV

Technology Related Assistance

In 1988 the Technology Related Assistance for Individuals with Disabilities Act, P.L. 100-409, 29 U.S.C. Sec. 2201 et seq., was enacted. Under this law the United States Department of Education National Institute on Disability and Rehabilitation Research makes grants to states to develop comprehensive statewide systems of resource information and assistive technology devices and services. The concept is to systemically synergize the major life function needs of consumers with technological information, services and devices. There is also a project to provide technical aid and information to the states' programs.

Enumerated below are the key points of contact in this program, which, as it grows, will facilitate more and more practical solutions to the problems encountered by persons with disabilities.

United States Department of Education

National Institute on Disability and Rehabilitation Research
400 Maryland Avenue, SW
Washington, D.C. 20202-2601
(202) 732-1141 (Voice); (202) 732-1198 (TDD)

RESNA Technical Assistance Project

1101 Connecticut Avenue, NW
Suite 700
Washington, D.C. 20036
(202) 857-1140 (Voice/TDD)

ALASKA

Division of Vocational Rehabilitation
Department of Education
P.O. Box F, M.S. 0581
Juneau, Alaska 99811-0500
(907) 465-2814

ARKANSAS

Department of Human Services
Division of Rehabilitation Services
P.O. Box 1437, Slot 2300
Little Rock, Arkansas 72203-1437
(501) 682-6689

COLORADO

Rocky Mountain Resource and Training Institute
3805 Marshall Street, Suite 202
Wheat Ridge, Colorado 80033
(303) 420-2942

ILLINOIS

Department of Rehabilitation Services
Division of Planning and Special Initiatives
623 E. Adams Street
P.O. Box 19429
Springfield, Illinois 62794-9429

INDIANA

Department of Human Services
Division of Rehabilitation Services
251 N. Illinois Street
P.O. Box 7083
Indianapolis, Indiana 46207-7083
(317) 232-1409

IOWA

University of Iowa
Division of Developmental Disabilities
Iowa City, Iowa 52242
(319) 353-6386

KENTUCKY

Kentucky Department for the Blind
427 Versailles Road
Frankfort, Kentucky 40601
(502) 564-4665

MAINE

Maine Department of Educational and Cultural Services
Division of Special Education
State House Station #23
Augusta, Maine 04333
(207) 289-5950

MARYLAND

Governor's Office for Handicapped Individuals
300 W. Lexington Street
1 Market Center, Box 10
Baltimore, Maryland 21201
(301) 333-3098

MASSACHUSETTS

Deputy Commissioner for Policy and Programs
Commission for the Deaf and Hard of Hearing
Central Office
600 Washington Street, Room 600
Boston, Massachusetts 02111
(617) 727-5106

MINNESOTA

Governor's Advisory Council for People with Disabilities
300 Centennial Building
685 Cedar Street
St. Paul, Minnesota 55155
(612) 297-1554

MISSISSIPPI

Division of Rehabilitation Services
Department of Human Services
P.O. Box 1698
Jackson, Mississippi 39215-1698
(601) 354-6272

NEBRASKA

Department of Education
Division of Rehabilitation Services
P.O. Box 94987
Lincoln, Nebraska 68509
(402) 471-3647

NEVADA

Rehabilitation Division, PRPD
505 East King Street, Room 502
Carson City, Nevada 89710
(702) 885-4440

NEW MEXICO

State Department of Education
Division of Vocational Rehabilitation
604 W. San Mateo
Santa Fe, New Mexico 87503
(505) 827-3522

NEW YORK

Office of the Advocate for the Disabled
One Empire Plaza
TRIAD Program
Albany, New York 12223-0001
(518) 474-2825, 473-4129

NORTH CAROLINA

Department of Human Resources
Division of Vocational Rehabilitation Services
P.O. Box 26053
Raleigh, North Carolina 27611
(919) 733-3364

OREGON

Department of Human Services
Vocational Rehabilitation Division
2045 Silverton Road, NE
Salem, Oregon 97310
(503) 378-3830

TENNESSEE

Developmental Disabilities Council
Department of Mental Health and Mental Retardation
Doctors' Building, Suite 300
706 Church Street
Nashville, Tennessee 37219
(615) 741-3807

UTAH

Utah State University
Developmental Center for Handicapped Persons
Logan, Utah 84322-6800
(801) 760-1982

VERMONT

Agency of Human Services
Planning Division
103 South Main Street
Waterbury, Vermont 05676
(802) 241-2228

VIRGINIA

Department of Rehabilitative Services
Office of Planning
4901 Fitzhugh Avenue
P.O. Box 11045
Richmond, Virginia 23230
(804) 367-0264

WISCONSIN

Department of Health and Social Services
Division of Vocational Rehabilitation
P.O. Box 7852
1 W. Wilson Street, 8th Floor
Madison, Wisconsin 53707
(608) 266-2179

ABOUT THE AUTHOR

CHARLES D. GOLDMAN is a Washington, D.C. attorney who has been actively engaged in disability issues and legislation for many years. A member of the Bars of the District of Columbia and the State of New York, Mr. Goldman has the perspective of a seasoned private practitioner with extensive government experience.

Mr. Goldman received the Book Award of the President's Committee on Employment of the Handicapped for the first edition of the *Disability Rights Guide*. He was the recipient of the Advocacy Award of the Epilepsy Foundation of America in 1988.

Charles D. Goldman served as the first General Counsel of the United States Architectural Transportation Barriers Compliance Board from 1975-1983. In that capacity he worked to develop national policies on disability issues and was one of the pioneer litigators on accessibility matters. Mr. Goldman also served as a LEGIS Fellow to Senator Carl Levin of Michigan.

Now in private practice, Mr. Goldman works with government agencies as well as private individuals and organizations to solve problems and develop policies and practices affecting persons with disabilities.

Mr. Goldman contributes regularly to professional journals. Mr. Goldman is a graduate of the University of Michigan. He received his J.D. from Brooklyn Law School and his L.L.M. from the New York University School of Law. He has also studied at Harvard Law School.

The Pinstripe Series

Disability Rights Guide: Practical Solutions to Problems Affecting People with Disabilities
Charles Goldman, J.D.

"Builds bridges of understanding between the business community and persons with disabilities. Excellent blend of the latest and relevant laws with clear, practical solutions!"

Tom Harkin
United States Senator

The second edition includes the most current information from the Americans with Disabilities Act of 1990 and the Fair Housing Amendments as well as updates on key state laws and expanded technology, discussions on attitudinal barriers, practical and legal information on employment, accessibility, housing, education, and transportation.

Goldman is a member of the District of Columbia and N.Y. State Bar Associations who specializes in disability rights issues.

Executive Guide to Employment Practices
A Practical Approach to Avoiding Unintended Discrimination
Thom K. Cope, J.D.

"...a clear, concise guide for managerial behavior, both for reasonable, equitable management practices and for avoidance of equal employment opportunity problems.... The book is very readable, not overly technical....Good preventative medicine."

Sarah E. Henry
Assistant VP, Irving Trust

Cope is a nationally respected authority in employment law and he conducts seminars throughout the U.S.; a member of the California, Nebraska and Federal Bar Associations.

How to Fire Your Friends
A Win-Win Approach to Effective Termination
Richard S. Deems, Ph.D.

"...a reasoned, human approach to terminating employees. ...Provides precise guidelines for the manager or employer who must do that distasteful of all duties: fire folks."

The Book Reader
San Francisco, CA

CEO of Deems Associates, Inc. with offices in Ames, IA and Scottsdale, AZ, Dr. Deems has worked with more than 9,000 persons in career-related issues since 1975.

ORDER DIRECT 1-800-36-MEDIA

☐ **YES**, I want ___ copies of **Disability Rights Guide** for $14.95 plus $2.50 shipping and handling.

☐ **YES**, I want ___ copies of **Executive Guide to Employment Practices** for $14.95 plus $2.50 shipping and handling.

☐ **YES**, I want ___ copies of **How to Fire Your Friends** for $14.95 plus $2.50 shipping and handling.

☐ **YES!** Send all 3 at a 25% Discount (plus $2.50 shipping and handling for the first book and $.50 each for additional book).

Method of payment

☐ Check for $_____ to:
Media Publishing
A Division of Westport Publishers, Inc.
2440 'O' Street
Suite 202
Lincoln, NE 68510

☐ Charge my credit card

   ☐ Visa   ☐ MasterCard

Account # _____

Exp. Date _____

Signature _____

Phone # _____

Ship to: _____

_____

_____

_____